Fitness
CROSS-COUNTRY
SKIING

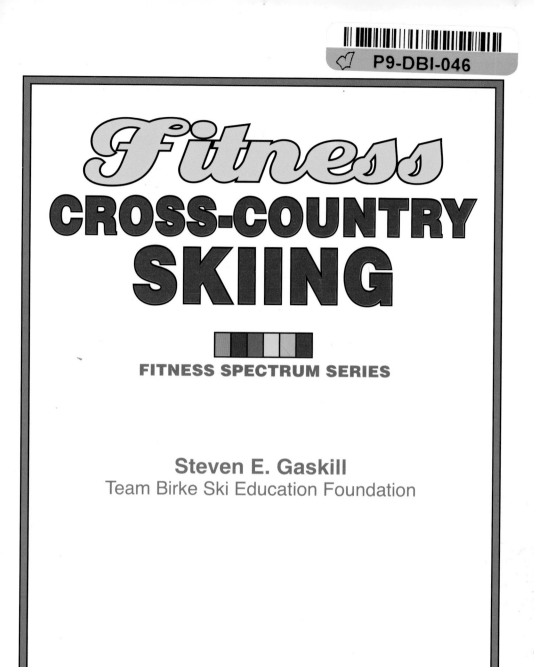

FITNESS SPECTRUM SERIES

Steven E. Gaskill
Team Birke Ski Education Foundation

Human Kinetics

Library of Congress Cataloging-in-Publication Data

Gaskill, Steven E., 1952–
    Fitness cross-country skiing / Steven E. Gaskill.
        p. cm. -- (Fitness spectrum series)
        ISBN 0-88011-652-8
        1. Cross-country skiing--Training. 2. Cross-country skiing. 3. Physical fitness.
    I. Title. II. Series.
    GV855.5.T73G37 1998
    796.93'2--dc21   97-16810
                                                                                    CIP

ISBN: 0-88011-652-8

Acquisitions Editor: Martin Barnard; **Developmental Editor:** Marni Basic; **Assistant Editor:** Henry Woolsey; **Editorial Assistant:** Amy Carnes; **Copyeditor:** Holly Gilly; **Proofreader:** Karen Bojda; **Graphic Designer:** Keith Blomberg; **Graphic Artist:** Doug Burnett; **Photo Editor:** Boyd LaFoon; **Cover Designer:** Jack Davis; **Photographer (cover):** John Kelly; **Illustrators:** Studio 2D

Human Kinetics books are available at special discounts for bulk purchase. Special editions or book excerpts can also be created to specification. For details, contact the Special Sales Manager at Human Kinetics.

Printed in Hong Kong 10 9 8 7 6 5 4 3 2 1

Human Kinetics
Web site: http://www.humankinetics.com/

United States: Human Kinetics, P.O. Box 5076, Champaign, IL 61825-5076
1-800-747-4457
e-mail: humank@hkusa.com

Canada: Human Kinetics, Box 24040, Windsor, ON N8Y 4Y9
1-800-465-7301 (in Canada only)
e-mail: humank@hkcanada.com

Europe: Human Kinetics, P.O. Box IW14, Leeds LS16 6TR, United Kingdom
(44) 1132 781708
e-mail: humank@hkeurope.com

Australia: Human Kinetics, 57A Price Avenue, Lower Mitcham, South Australia 5062
(08) 277 1555
e-mail: humank@hkaustralia.com

New Zealand: Human Kinetics, P.O. Box 105-231, Auckland 1
(09) 523 3462
e-mail: humank@hknewz.com

This book is dedicated to all of the great cross-country skiers who have enriched my life with their love of skiing and their drive to excel. My thanks also to my family, who have allowed me to give much of my life to cross-country skiing at their expense, yet have continued to come out with me and share the quiet beauty of gliding along. Thanks.

Contents

PART I

PREPARING FOR CROSS-COUNTRY SKIING

To cross-country ski is to dance on snow. From the recreational skier knee deep in white fluff to the competitive racer floating over a manicured course, cross-country skiing gives the freedom to enjoy the outdoors in winter. For the elite skier, it is poetry in motion; for the fitness enthusiast, it is a blend of nature and exercise.

Cross-country skiing has long been recognized as an activity that requires some of the highest levels of endurance on the fitness spectrum. Like cycling and swimming, it doesn't jar the body. It is a whole-body workout that uses more muscles than nearly any other sport. It can be done as a family or individually, at a high speed or at a gentle glide through the snow. It will strengthen your body, improve your cardiovascular fitness, and help you build the mind-body relationship for a healthy life.

Many top athletes turn to cross-country skiing during the winter to stay fit. Cyclists, runners, triathletes, and swimmers are seen out on the trails during the winter. Alpine skiers use cross-country as a way to maintain an endurance base and hone their balance skills.

Although cross-country skiing is a winter activity, make it a part of your broader, year-round fitness program. This book is written with that in mind: It stresses variety. As you move through the chapters, you will be led through a systematic development of an activity regimen that will help you lead a healthy and productive life, feel good about your body, and be vigorous in your lifestyle. No matter what your current activity level, *Fitness Cross-Country Skiing* will help you design a program to maintain and improve your fitness, one stride at a time.

In the chapters in part I, I'll examine cross-country skiing as part of a total fitness program—winter, spring, summer, and fall.

Chapter 1 takes a look at the benefits of cross-country skiing for those getting started, for fitness enthusiasts, and for endurance athletes. You'll learn about the individual needs and requirements for different levels of fitness and participation, from endurance and strength to flexibility and mental skills. The chapter ends with a section to help you set goals in your fitness and cross-country skiing program.

Chapter 2 describes the clothing, skis, boots, poles, and other items you need for safe and fun participation, no matter whether you plan on touring in a city park or a snowy field or on doing some high-speed cross-country ski skating on prepared trails. I offer some guidelines about equipment quality and price, and I help you consider the special needs associated with winter activities.

Chapter 3 shows you how to do a personal inventory of your strengths and weaknesses. This inventory helps you determine what program level to begin with. It also helps you identify special areas for improving and maintaining your fitness.

Chapter 4 is a primer of the techniques of cross-country skiing. I teach you the basics of positions and timing, terminology for effective touring, and track techniques. I also cover how to vary your training exercises and how training methods, intensity, and duration all interact to give you the training effects you desire.

Chapter 5 reviews the best methods of preparing for and finishing each training session. It includes a set of stretches for the postexercise period of your workout to keep you lithe and flexible.

Get ready for a wonderful winter adventure. You have taken the first step. The rest just gets better.

Skiing for Fitness

In the snowbelt, winter can be a blessing or a bane to the endurance athlete. For runners, bikers, rowers, triathletes, and swimmers, usual outdoor training activities may become greatly curtailed, if not completely eliminated. For those outfitted with cross-country ski gear, however, the winter becomes an exquisitely delightful playground, and winter exercise again becomes a joy. Cross-country skiing allows athletes and fitness enthusiasts to maintain fitness through the cold months, adding upper-body power and endurance, increasing aerobic capacity, and developing a balanced leg power that seems to enhance all other sports.

In 1976, Bill Koch stunned winter sport enthusiasts by being the first American to win a medal in cross-country skiing at the Winter Olympics. A few years later, in 1981, he won the World Cup title by using a skating technique that he witnessed while skating in marathon races. Cross-country skiing hasn't been the same since. With the advent of ski skating, along with the traditional "classic" technique, cross-country skiing offers a wide variety of activities, from the pleasure of touring in untracked snow to the abandon of high-speed ski skating on well-groomed trails.

Cross-country skiing is a sport that can provide lifetime enjoyment. Youth leagues around the country offer skiing for youngsters as young as 5 years, and races for masters often have competitors 70 years and older. A few years ago, while I was backcountry touring with friends in Colorado, I met a group of elderly skiers near the top of remote Hagerman Pass, enjoying life as much as I was.

Opportunities for hut touring (skiing from one backcountry hut to another), or simply for skiing to one hut and staying for several days, are growing rapidly. The network of maintained trails continues to grow in number and quality. In short, if you live where it snows, like the outdoors, and enjoy exercise, you are in for a treat at whatever level you choose to participate.

© John Kelly

Cross-country skiing is a sport for all ages.

Who Skis?

Men and women participate in cross-country skiing in equal numbers. Likewise, an even distribution of ages is represented in the cross-country skiing population. The number of adults beginning cross-country skiing as a fitness activity has been steadily rising over the past decade, and ski programs in high schools in the snowbelt states are growing, too. Cross-country skiing continues to attract new participants, and with more ski areas dedicated to providing groomed trails and equipment manufacturers improving their products, the sport is likely to maintain its popularity as a fitness and family activity.

Most skiers, naturally, come from states with snow and trails. The upper Midwest—Minnesota, Wisconsin, and Michigan—supports the largest population of skiers, with the New England states and New York close behind. The mountain states provide wonderful cross-country ski areas, a network of programs and races, a long season, and wonderful snow. The Pacific coastal mountains in Washington, Oregon, and California also have great skiing and skiing organizations. There are, however, people who live all over the United States who travel to snow to do their skiing or who simulate cross-country ski training with roller skis (cross-country skis with wheels to use on pavement), hike with poles, and use other methods of training the appropriate muscles for cross-country skiing. The American Birkebeiner, the largest cross-country ski event in North America, regularly draws participants from nearly all 50 states.

Cross-country skiers come in all sizes, shapes, and abilities. They have learned to love the winter outdoors and the wind on their faces. Cross-country skiers also quickly learn that their sport provides the best aerobic fitness training, leads to better overall body fitness, burns a lot of calories, and is a body-friendly activity that can be enjoyed alone or with friends and family for a lifetime.

Why Ski?

Cross-country skiing activates more muscles than most other sports, which results in improvements to circulation and the ability of the heart to pump more blood. These training effects carry over to all other sports, making cross-country skiing a great winter alternative for running, cycling, rowing, swimming, and all other aerobic sports.

Consider these benefits:

- Cross-country skiing doesn't pound your joints, and it gives your legs a break from running-related stresses.

- Your arms and legs get a great workout. Cross-country skiing is a great way to strengthen your upper body, and it helps to compensate for lifestyles that tend not to use the upper body and arms.
- Cross-country skiing is less expensive than downhill skiing though good equipment is well worth the investment. Most afficionados can find their fun near home, so they don't need to spend vacation money to get to a cross-country ski destination.
- It is an efficient way to get fitness benefits. The physical benefits for the time you spend are very high. You can maintain or improve your fitness with as little as one or two hours of skiing per week.
- Everyone is welcome. Nearly all events are open to all ages and abilities. You can be a part of the same race as champions, and feel like a champion yourself.
- You can participate alone or with a group, at a high speed or on an easy tour, on easy trails or in challenging terrain. You can usually even ski on a schedule that fits your free time, day or night.

Cross-country skiing does have a few shortcomings that all participants need to be aware of:

- Snow can be unreliable, as can the weather. We expect nature to cooperate, but winter can sometimes bring some harsh surprises. Participants need to be prepared.
- Injuries can happen, although they're rare. Cross-country skiers experience 10 percent fewer strains, sprains, and other injuries than alpine, or downhill, skiers do. Cold-related injuries are more common, but you can avoid them easily. Preparation and good clothing, along with smart choices about the trail levels you attempt, minimize risk. Cross-country skiing can boast one of the lowest injury rates of all sports.
- The equipment requires some care and, depending on your needs and desires, it can be expensive. You need to wax your skis and occasionally the ski bases may need professional care. You will also need appropriate clothing, boots, and poles.
- Skiing exercises a great many muscles but, like any activity, muscle imbalances can occur. Make a well-rounded fitness program a part of your ski program. (This book will help you develop a well-rounded program.)
- Cross-country skiing requires that you attain a certain level of skill development to become proficient. This book covers the basics, but video instruction, books on ski technique, or lessons will greatly enhance your cross-country skiing pleasure.

Skiing Your Way to Health and Fitness

Cross-country skiing and the training associated with it can be worked into a balanced program that will provide full fitness benefits. No single activity can provide the multiple and varying fitness needs of all individuals, but a combination of training can provide you with the strength, power, endurance, coordination, and improved body composition that will give you a foundation of sound training to help you in all of your other sports and in your daily life. Cross-country ski training incorporates many of the aspects of cross-training to simulate the muscular and endurance needs of cross-country skiing, even when there is no snow on the ground.

Here's how cross-country skiing affects five components of fitness:

- **Cardiovascular fitness and health:** This is the ability of your heart and circulation system to deliver blood and nutrients to the working muscles and organs within your body. Cross-country skiing, because of the large number of muscles used, is believed to be one of the very best sports in improving your cardiovascular fitness. Even easy tours will raise your heart rate

© Mountain Stock/Bob Woodward

Cross-country skiing can be a great social sport.

to 60 percent to 70 percent of maximum. Two or three times a week for 20 to 30 minutes will help to increase the amount of blood your heart can pump. This is a primary factor in fitness for endurance sports. As you exercise more, you will develop increased numbers of capillaries in your working muscles, which increases your blood flow. More capillaries will also lower the resistance to blood flow and will help to lower your blood pressure. An increased red blood cell count means more oxygen-carrying capacity and a greater oxygen supply to your heart and muscles. All of this means increased cardiovascular fitness and a reduction in the risk of heart and vascular disease. Higher-intensity or longer-duration exercise will increase the benefits as long as they are balanced with appropriate rest and low-intensity exercise.

- **Muscular endurance:** This is the ability of specific muscles to withstand long periods of exercise or work without fatiguing. The intensity of exercise will generally determine how fast a muscle fatigues. Endurance training greatly increases the aerobic capacity of the muscles so that they can get a great deal more energy from food sources than if the work is done anaerobically (without oxygen). The difference is about 18 times more energy when the energy sources are burned with oxygen. Also, fat can be used as an energy source only when oxygen is available. Muscular endurance thus applies to the increases in the muscle's ability to use oxygen. With aerobic training and repeated use, this ability goes up and muscles become more aerobically fit and can withstand greater loads for sustained periods. Cross-country skiing provides a great training method to increase the muscular endurance of many muscles. Improving muscular endurance for some muscles may require strength training with light to medium weights and high repetition.

- **Muscular strength:** Strength provides the ability to move objects or to produce power. All sport events require some strength with the more explosive sports requiring greater strength and power. Cross-country skiing, especially ski skating, which is thought of as a power-endurance sport, requires a moderately high level of strength to develop the forceful skating strokes and the strong poling motion required for fluid ski skating. Increases in strength will provide you protection from injury of muscles and joints, give you more confidence in all physical activities, and help you maintain a better muscle and bone mass as you age. Some strength training will enhance your cross-country skiing ability. Cross-country skiing requires the use of the greatest number of different muscles. Major muscles of the arms, including the triceps, rotator cuffs, pecs, deltoids, and lats, receive the benefit of ski training. Abdominal and back muscles, along with major leg muscles including the quads, hamstrings, gastrocnemius, abductors, adductors, soleus, and anterior tibialis, are all used extensively and will enjoy greater aerobic endurance and muscular strength through cross-country skiing.

- **Flexibility:** Good flexibility allows you to use your full range of motion without the need to overcome resistance from tight muscles or joints. It also gives a cushion of protection from injury should you fall and overextend a joint. As you train, especially when you use muscles that are not well trained, it is common for muscles to get tight. Daily flexibility routines will help you to maintain and increase your range of motion. Decreased flexibility comes with age, particularly to men after age 30. Decreased flexibility increases the risk of injury. However, stretching is recommended for all ages to maintain a supple body. Ski training does not naturally give your muscles much stretch, and overall flexibility may decrease. Stretch before and after all workouts.

- **Body composition:** Body composition is largely a factor of the exercise you do, the quantity of calories you consume, and the total calories you expend. Body composition is expressed in terms of body fat and lean body mass (everything that is not fat). In simple terms, your body stores as fat nearly all the extra calories beyond what you expend for daily life and exercise. Excess fat is unhealthy and will hinder your ability to participate in sports. Cross-country skiing provides an excellent mechanism for burning extra calories.

Based on data from physically active young adults, average body fat values of 15 percent for men and 25 percent for women provide good values to serve as a frame of reference. As you age, there will be a gradual increase in body fat and a loss of lean body mass. However for very fit endurance athletes this range is more likely to be 8 percent to 15 percent for men and 12 percent to 25 percent for women. A lifetime regimen of aerobic activity is particularly effective in reducing body fat, because it improves the aerobic fitness of one's muscles and their ability to burn fat as an energy source. The variety of training for cross-country skiing will allow you to be active every day. Consider that if you do 20 minutes of easy aerobic activity a day, or the equivalent of two miles of walking, that will equal about 200 calories a day or about 30 pounds of fat a year as long as you don't change your eating habits. Endurance activities don't cause you to lose weight quickly, but you will slowly lose fat, develop muscle, and over time you will begin a drop of about a half pound or more a week until you reach a new equilibrium. By that time you will be feeling really fit and will be able to go at a slightly higher intensity or go for a longer duration.

The Basics of Training

All coaches and athletes in aerobic (endurance) activities follow the same general fundamentals in outlining their training. The three big questions for training are: How hard? How often? How long? These three are usually referred to as intensity (how hard to train), frequency (how often to train), and duration (how long to train each session). Exercise must be balanced with recovery. Training requires a fine line between too little (with no improvements) and too much (resulting in injury and poor results). I will discuss these issues in more depth later on.

Training for endurance sports, including cross-country skiing, can be separated into three general categories. Part III contains sample programs for each category. Each category uses its own duration, frequency, and intensity guidelines.

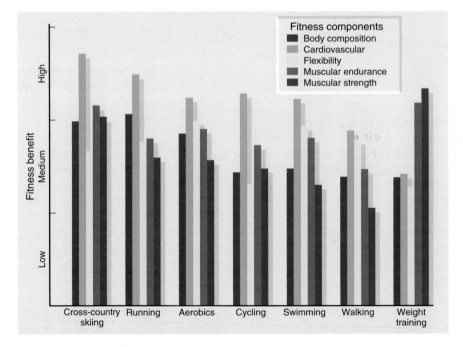

How cross-country skiing compares to other sports.

- **Basic fitness and maintenance:** Easy cross-country skiing and touring to promote health and basic fitness, or to maintain a moderate level of aerobic fitness. In this book the basic programs are for those who are interested in maintaining aerobic fitness through the winter via cross-country skiing. The programs are not for those interested in racing or pushing their personal limits. These programs contain three to four days a week, which include skiing and other exercises, with an average time of about 20 to 40 minutes (a few longer workouts are recommended), and there's never more than one hard activity a week.
- **Moderate fitness and improvement:** Doing enough to improve so that you can begin to participate in some of the more dynamic components of cross-country skiing and venture out onto more hills and longer adventures. The moderate fitness programs include activities three to five days a week averaging 25 to 50 minutes with one hard activity a week and some longer aerobic activities.
- **Competitive/high-intensity skiing:** For those who want to race and become competitive in their age groups. It requires a dedication to training of five to seven days a week, averaging about 45 to 60 minutes a day with some longer skis, and one or two hard sessions a week.

Other Training Activities

Cross-country skiers use a wide variety of activities to train during the spring, summer, and fall. For many skiers, the summer activities are their primary sports, and they use skiing during the winter to improve their cardiovascular fitness. Whatever your reasons for cross-country skiing, you will find that a multitude of activities will benefit your skiing, facilitate a full-body fitness program, and give variety and interest to your training.

Even during the winter, most cross-country skiers do some other activities such as jogging, swimming, and light strength exercises. Some of the more prominent activities that cross-country skiers do include running, swimming, cycling and mountain biking, hiking with poles, strength and resistance training, circuit training, roller boarding, workouts on cross-country ski simulators, in-line skating, roller skiing, and hill bounding.

Chapter 2 provides a description of the equipment needed for these activities and chapter 4 provides a description of how to do each of the activities. Of course, not everyone desires to become a super athlete and it isn't necessary that you do everything. Just pick a few of your favorite activities, or branch out into one or two new ones, and then use the workouts in this book to design your program.

The biggest step in becoming involved in cross-country skiing is simply deciding it fits your needs and is a sport you would like to try. Getting the basic equipment and walking out the door for your first adventure is the next step.

Getting Equipped

You have a choice: You can be an equipment junkie or just buy the basics. As a former serious competitor and ski coach, I definitely fit into the equipment junkie class, with more than 10 pairs of skis, several boots, hundreds of different waxes, training equipment. . . . I could outfit and provide training equipment for a full team. You can keep it a lot simpler.

Whichever choice you make, you will need to focus on function and safety. What you need to purchase depends on your level and what type of skiing you will do. There is also the question of the training equipment for all of the other possible activities that cross-country skiers can do to maintain their fitness when there is no snow around. You may already own a lot of the simple gear needed for the nonskiing portion of the year.

Cross-Country Ski Equipment

As a general guideline, try to get high-quality equipment at every level. You will enjoy your skiing time much more, develop more quickly, and avoid equipment problems and even injury.

Skis, boots, bindings, and poles are the main essentials to start with. Use the information in this section to help you start to consider the right type of equipment, and then visit a reputable ski shop that has a good inventory of cross-country ski gear. If you don't have access to a local ski shop, consider ordering from one of the good mail-order firms that are available. It is beyond the scope of this book to go into the many details of ski, boot, and binding selection, but I'll provide a few things for you to think about if you're making your first purchase. Be aware that boots and bindings usually come as matched sets. That is, each type of boot requires the correct binding system, and when you replace boots you will need to buy some that fit your current bindings, or you'll need to replace boots and bindings both. Because of this, it is best to stick with the major manufacturers.

Skis

If you are just starting out, decide if you plan to ski primarily on packed trails, in the backcountry, or a combination of both. If you plan to ski primarily on packed trails, decide if you want to do ski skating, classic technique, or both. All of these things will influence the kinds of skis you'll purchase.

A second important consideration is whether to purchase skis that have a waxable base (meaning you apply kick wax for classic technique) or no-wax bases (meaning the base has a fishscale or other pattern ground into it that allows you to glide forward but not to slip backward). Waxable bases are best if you live in an area with cold, dry snow for most of the year. No-wax bases are great for climates with lots of wet or moist snow and rapidly changing conditions. I'll return to these issues later when I talk about costs.

Boots

Boots are the major component to successful cross-country skiing, even if skis get most of the attention. Boots need to fit well and provide adequate warmth for the activity. For skating, the boots also need to provide good ankle support. The major brands are very reliable for support and warmth, but try them on for fit because the width of each brand differs and your comfort is at stake. Racing boots tend to be lighter with less insulation, but on cold days racers wear overboots or boot muffs to provide extra warmth. Boots for touring should have moderate insulation and enough room to fit well with two pairs of thin wool socks. Boots that don't fit well or don't give good support and control to the skis ultimately result in an unpleasant ski experience.

Poles

Poles need to be the correct size and type for their intended function. The length that's appropriate for each activity varies, as does the size of the pole basket that keeps the pole from sinking into the snow. Racing poles are longer and stiffer than touring poles, and they need to be very light and stiff and to have small baskets. Skating poles are longer than classic technique poles. Price also varies greatly, and the price of top-end poles increases quickly as they get lighter.

Clothing

Gloves and socks protect your extremities and a hat will prevent large losses of heat from your head. The type of cross-country skiing activity you do will greatly affect your decision. When you visit a store or browse through a catalogue, be sure that you know what kind of skiing you plan to do.

Socks

It is often nice to have a very thin polypropylene sock next to the skin to wick away moisture. An outer sock should be wool or a mostly wool blend. Multiple layers of thin socks are more comfortable, and allow for better temperature and fit adjustment, than bulky socks.

Gloves

Your choice of gloves also depends on temperature and activity. Here again, the layer principle gives the greatest flexibility. The combination of a thin polypropylene liner glove, a lightweight cross-country glove or mitt (large enough to go over your hand and the liner) plus a pair of outer mitts (thinly insulated and loose fitting) will be a combination that you can mix and match to fit any condition, from the warm sunny day to very cold temperatures.

Hats

The more vigorous the activity, the lighter the hat you need. Again, wool is the best choice, but a sewn-in polypropylene sweatband adds comfort and dryness. Lightweight cross-country skiing earmuffs, which go right under a hat, add a final layer of protection for sensitive ears on cold days, and they can be worn alone on warmer days. You lose a great deal of heat through your head, and a very light hat or headband may be adequate if you're working hard. On warm days you may choose to wear no hat. However, be careful of windchill and hypothermia. If you are chilled, be sure to keep a hat on, and keep your earlobes covered if they have a tendency to freeze easily as mine do.

Choose your cross-country ski clothing based on your likes and dislikes. Lycra suits are the norm for the racing crowd, but looser pants and tops are becoming more popular and most people find them more comfortable. Use the layering principle: Wear several thin layers rather than a few bulky layers, placing wicking layers such as polypropylene close to the skin. Polypropylene, or one of the new softer synthetics like Capilene, Prolite, Drylete, or synthetic meshes that wick the moisture away from your body, is always a good first layer. What you wear over the long underwear is up to you. More experienced tourers seem to prefer moderately loose-fitting tights with a turtleneck top. On cold or windy days, they usually wear a breathable windproof top over a fleece jacket and a pair of breathable windproof pants.

© Dennis G. Hendricks

A wide variety of equipment is available for cross-country skiing, depending on your needs and goals.

Accessories

Don't venture out without these items:

- Sunglasses and sunscreen are essential for sunny days. Eyewear helps keep the snowflakes out of your eyes on a long downhill run when it's snowing.
- A high-quality headlamp with a halogen bulb and rechargeable batteries is a great asset if you want to ski at night on unlighted trails.
- Carry a small pack and water bottle if you are going for more than a very short tour. Plan for the outing by anticipating needs and potential problems, considering the weather, and the length of your trip. Pack a dry hat, extra kick wax and a cork if you are skiing classic technique, a windshell, and dry gloves. If you plan to be out for more than an hour, carry some energy snacks and a small, insulated thermos (to keep your fluids from freezing). I love a warm, sweetened tea during a long tour.

Costs

It'll cost more for you to get started in cross-country skiing than it will to maintain your gear every year. Eventually, you'll replace your skis or get better equipment as you gain skill and learn what you really want. The prices that follow are estimates for average gear. I recommend that you get decent equipment to begin with. Of course, you can get top-of-the-line equipment; you'll pay about twice the listed price for it. Remember to budget for trail fees in your area. They may vary from a minimal annual trail fee, such as the $8 family pass in Minnesota, to daily fees charged at most privately run areas. My experience is that these fees are very reasonable, especially when compared to fees for alpine skiing and for other sport activities. The cost of maintaining trails can be quite high where there is lots of snow groomed with high-tech equipment.

Costs for skis, boots and bindings, poles, and wax will vary, depending on the kind of skiing you plan to do. To give you an idea of what your decisions about on- or off-trail touring and ski skating or classic technique skiing mean in terms of what you spend, I've described costs in terms of four categories that take into account these differences.

> **EQUIPMENT TIP** In climates where the snow tends to be cold and dry (where air temperatures are often under 20 degrees Fahrenheit), waxable bases will give much better performance, and they're easy to wax. In climates like the Pacific Northwest where the snow is often wet and sticky, no-wax bases usually work better.

- **Combination on- and off-trail touring:** An abundance of light touring equipment is available for touring on groomed trails or easy terrain off of the beaten path. This equipment will work well for easy ski tours using classic technique, but don't expect to be able to skate on skis that also work off-trail. Ask specifically for light touring skis that can be used off-trail. Poles should have large baskets designed for soft snow and be about 80 percent of skier's height. When choosing boots, think first about warmth and fit for classic skiing. Typical package prices for skis, boots, bindings, and poles range from $250 to $350.

- **Off-trail skiing:** For off-trail skiing (short tours without emergency equipment), your equipment will depend on where you plan to go. I base my recommendations here on gentle terrain without large uphills or downhills. Look for equipment similar to the previous category, but look for medium to heavy touring skis designed solely for off-trail use ($200 to $250). In addition, look for heavier and warmer boots ($150-$250) and heavier bindings ($50 to $75). Work with a reputable shop or mail-order business for sizing and fit. I also recommend gaiters to keep the snow out of your boots. Poles ($50) should be designed for backcountry, have large baskets, and be about 80 percent of your height. Equipment recommendations for backcountry skiing are beyond the scope of this book. Don't approach a trip into the mountains, or even out for an all-day tour, casually. Such excursions require experience, knowledge of avalanche conditions, and route-finding, survival, and good skiing skills. Expect to spend $450 to $600 for good equipment that will work well and get you back home.

- **Ski skating:** Ski skating requires packed trails. It's better to buy special skating skis than to try to skate on waxable classic skis; it is nearly impossible to skate on no-wax skis. If you want to ski skate, start with good equipment. Get skis that are designed for your weight and ability. Work with a good shop or mail-order business to get a good fit. Ski companies are making skating skis in several lengths. For beginners, skis that are about your height are easier to learn on and will work well as long as the snow is well packed. If you usually ski on soft snow, look for "powder skis" that are a little longer (about 10 centimeters longer) and have a little softer flex. Expect to pay between $250 and $300 for reasonable skating skis. The price will be worth it! Poles for skating also need to be stiffer and longer (about 88 to 90 percent of body height) than classic or backcountry poles. You can expect to pay between $100 and $150 for good beginner poles,

Cross-country skiing is an exhilarating sport.

but it's worth it. Ski skating boots provide more ankle support than other cross-country boots and range in price from about $100 to $200. A typical skating package will cost between $500 and $600 for skis, boots, bindings, and poles.

- **Classic skiing or skate-classic combo package for packed trails:** This category offers the greatest possibility for a wide range of equipment, from walking on skis to higher performance with good kick and glide. As always, I recommend getting good equipment to begin with. You will learn faster, enjoy it more, have better control, and probably ski more frequently. Classic skis are usually about 110 percent to 112 percent of body height. More important than length is flex, which is determined by your weight, your experience, and the typical snow that you ski on (wet, icy, or powdery). Work with a reputable ski shop or mail-order business to get a pair of skis that will fit you well. If you want a combination skate-classic ski or strictly a classic ski, look for a major brand and plan to buy one of the midpriced skis. Poles for classic should be about 85 percent of body height or, for a pair of combination poles, about 87 percent. Boots also come in classic-only or combination boots. A typical package price for skis, boots, poles, and bindings is about $400 to $500.

Training Gear

What you spend on gear for training activities other than skiing is up to you. Your expenses can be as varied as your imagination (if you plan to cycle, roller ski, or in-line skate), or as simple as running shoes, shorts, and a T-shirt. Start simple and then add clothing, equipment, tools, and toys as necessary and desired.

ADDING UP THE COSTS

In addition to your package price you may want a few additional items. Even if you buy no-wax skis, you should plan to buy glide wax because all skis need occasional glide waxing. If you purchased waxable skis you will also need kick wax.

KICK WAX	$	20-75
GLIDE WAX		25-75
WAXING TOOLS		
(WAXING IRON AND		
WAX SCRAPERS)		25-100
LONG UNDERWEAR		60
CROSS-COUNTRY SKI PANTS		60
WIND PANTS		60
TURTLENECK		30
FLEECE JACKET		75
WIND TOP		60
SOCKS, POLYPRO (2 PAIR)		15
SOCKS, WOOL (2 PAIR)		15
HAT		21
GLOVES		
LINERS		8
GLOVES		30
OVERMITTS		12
SMALL PACK OR		
WATER BOTTLE PACK		35
TOTAL COSTS		
(INCLUDING SKI PACKAGE)	$	751-1,331

Tips for Training in a Winter Climate

Cross-country skiing provides a wonderful opportunity to continue your aerobic training year 'round. If the weather is reasonable, it is great to head outdoors for a bit of refreshing exercise. If the weather is really cold, or if skiing is not possible, there are lots of things that you can do indoors to help your skiing or maintain your fitness for other activities. However, most ski enthusiasts rejoice in cold weather and new snow. Beware; cross-country skiing can become addicting, and you may find that you can't wait to get your skis on the snow, regardless of the conditions. Our club occasionally even straps on our skis in the middle of summer to run up and down grassy slopes on a rainy day. (The rain makes the grass a little slippery.)

Training outdoors in the winter requires some preparation and planning. It is important to pay attention to the weather forecasts and to be prepared for worse weather and lower temperatures than predicted. Frostbite, especially of the extremities, and hypothermia (low body temperature and loss of body heat) cause the greatest injuries to cross-country skiers. The estimated injury rate in cross-country skiing is quite low at about 1.5 to 2 per 1,000 skiers in Minnesota, and several studies have reported injury rates in cross-country as being between only 10 percent to 27 percent of those reported in alpine or downhill skiing. However, since the 1970s brought faster synthetic skies and bases, more cross-country skiing injuries are being reported related to collisions with other skiers, with trees, and from falls, though most injuries are minor abrasions and bruises.

It is also important, just as it is in any other season, to drink fluids while training in the winter. That can be difficult, because water bottles can freeze up. Here are some ideas to help you prepare for winter training:

- Always prepare for colder weather than you are expecting. Using the layer system, you can always easily adjust.
- When the temperature dips lower than 10 degrees, be extra careful of exposed skin and your earlobes and nose. Wear an extra layer on your hands and feet. The international rule for races is that they must be canceled when the temperature is below –1 degree Fahrenheit. Use your common sense. If there is a chance that you will get frostbite, stay in or dress really warmly and go very slowly.
- Take a small fanny pack with you and carry a light wind top and wind pants if you are going far.
- Always let someone know where you are going and when you expect to be back, especially on off-trail outings.

- When you go fast and at a high intensity, you'll produce more heat, and you'll find that you don't need to wear a lot of layers. In fact, if you wear too much, you will sweat and then become chilled. However, when you are going very hard on a cold day, you must still wear overmitts, earmuffs, and maybe even overboots. You may feel hot, but your extremities can still freeze very quickly.
- Know the route that you are going to ski. Stay within your ability and take it easy on downhills until you are confident of your ability.
- Take a water bottle (preferably the insulated kind) with you in a fanny pack or take a small backpack along with some snacks or energy bars.
- Ski with a partner if you are going off-trail.
- Lock your car and leave no valuables in it. Many trail heads are now the targets of thieves.
- If you are classic skiing, take a tube of cold snow wax and a tube of warm snow wax, plus a cork to smooth out the wax should your ski require rewaxing due to a temperature change or the old wax wearing off.
- Bring a change of dry clothes, or at least a dry T-shirt, with you to change into after your exercise is done. This really helps you avoid chills and you will feel much more comfortable.
- Stretch regularly and pay special attention to your hamstrings after cross-country skiing.
- Use extreme caution on icy trails, downhills, and corners.

© Mountain Stock/John Clausen

Clothing for cross-country skiing tends to be functional and lightweight, using a system of several light layers that can be adjusted rather than a few heavy layers of clothing.

3

Checking Your Skiing Fitness Level

The old adage "If you can walk, you can ski" may not be entirely true, but it's close. In its simplest form, cross-country skiing is no more than walking on skis while using poles for balance. However, as you begin to learn good ski technique, the skis glide and the poles apply arm power to keep your skis gliding. Also, most trails are not completely flat, and many require that you are able to go a minimal distance to ski around a loop. It is important to evaluate your fitness before you get started so that you can begin a training program at an appropriate level. Regardless of your fitness, there is a program for you in cross-country skiing and an exciting world of winter exercise for you to experience.

The other important training consideration is your current health status. Your health and fitness are independent factors that need to be evaluated separately. Three tests on the following pages will help you (1) decide whether you should first see a doctor before beginning an exercise program, (2) test your program readiness, and (3) test your aerobic fitness with a 1.5-mile walk/run test. If you're honest with yourself, the results will help you find an appropriate level at which to begin your training. Overestimating your abilities or ignoring health issues may result in your choosing an inappropriate program, which will lead to poor results, including possible pain or injury.

When you have finished the two questionnaires that follow and have done the 1.5-mile run/walk test, you will have a good starting point for your training. I'll use this information in part III to give you an idea about how to begin training and which programs to follow.

Assessing Your Physical Readiness

If you answer yes to any of the questions in the following preparation checklist, you should see a physician before beginning a training program.

PREPARATION CHECKLIST

		Yes	No
1.	Do you have a history of heart disease, vascular disease, or blood clots?	___	___
2.	Are you under the care of a physician for any heart or circulatory condition?	___	___
3.	Do you have diabetes and take insulin to control it?	___	___
4.	Do you take any daily medication that may be affected by exercise?	___	___
5.	Are you over 45 and have you not exercised over the past 5 years?	___	___
6.	Are you currently undergoing rehabilitation for an occupational or accident-related injury?	___	___
7.	Do you smoke 10 or more cigarettes a day?	___	___
8.	Is there a history of heart disease in your family, and have you not been exercising or have you been exercising infrequently?	___	___
9.	Have you noticed a shortness of breath or light-headedness after any sustained aerobic exertion, such as riding a stationary bike for 20 or more minutes? (This does not apply to anaerobic exertion like sprinting or running up and down a basketball court.)	___	___

(continued)

10. Do you have chronic orthopedic problems, arthritis, or other metabolic diseases?   ____ ____

11. Are you pregnant, and have you not been exercising prior to or at all during pregnancy?   ____ ____

Testing Your Program Readiness

Because cross-country ski training can involve a nearly limitless selection of activities, your test of readiness may vary considerably, depending on the nature of fitness you wish to achieve. The checklist that follows is designed to help you interpret your cardiovascular fitness and readiness for a training program. In each of the seven areas, choose the number that best describes you. At the end, you will total your answers.

ASSESSING YOUR CROSS-COUNTRY SKIING READINESS

Current activity

Fill in the number of hours and partial hours that you participate each week in the following activities:

	Hours	
Aerobic sports like running, biking, rowing, hiking, in-line skating	____ x 6 =	_____
Any other sports like basketball, soccer, racquetball, alpine skiing	____ x 5 =	_____
Strength training	____ x 5 =	_____

Subtotal for activity: _____

Injury profile

Choose the number that best describes the frequency with which you have had the following injuries: 1 (yes, frequently), 2 (sometimes or have in the past), 3 (rarely or never)

Do you get foot or ankle injuries?   ____

Do you get upper-body or shoulder injuries?   ____

Do you have lower back problem?   ____

Subtotal for injuries: _____

(continued)

Weight status

Which of these statements best describes your current weight?

You are within 10 pounds of your ideal weight. _____(3)

You are 11 to 19 pounds over or under your ideal weight. _____(2)

You are 20 pounds or more over or under your ideal weight. _____(1)

Age

Which age category describes you?

Age 30 or less _____(5)
Age 31- 40 _____(4)
Age 41- 50 _____(3)
Age 51- 60 _____(2)
Age 61 and over _____(1)

Resting pulse

What is your resting pulse (your heart rate after waking in the morning, but before getting out of bed)?

Below 60 beats per minute _____(4)
60 to 69 beats per minute _____(3)
70 to 75 beats per minute _____(2)
76 or more beats per minute _____(1)

Cardiovascular health

Which statement best describes your cardiovascular history?

No history of heart or circulatory problems _____(3)
Past conditions now treated and reversed _____(2)
Heart and circulatory problems self-monitored _____(1)

Smoking status

Which statement best describes you?

Never smoke, or have quit at least 12 months ago _____(4)
Sometimes smoke _____(1)
Smoke at least 10 cigarettes a day _____(0)

Total score: _____

After determining your total score, use the following scales to inter-pret your score. Remember, if you answered yes to any of the prepa-ration checklist questions, you should still check with your physician before starting a program.

More than 55—You have excellent readiness for cardiovascular and cross-country ski training. You can begin with workouts in any of the training zones.

37-54—You have moderate readiness for cardiovascular and cross-country ski training. You should consider starting training in the Green through Yellow zones.

26-36—You need to exercise caution in planning your activities. Start with the easiest workouts and be sure to keep the intensity of train-ing at low levels, adding more time at low intensities before adding harder workouts. Consider beginning your workouts with training in the Green and Blue zones.

Less than 25—It is best for you to seek professional advice and assis-tance in planning your program. If you answered no to all questions in the preparation checklist and feel that you are able to begin a training program, consider starting with only Green zone workouts and then progressing to other zones as your fitness level increases.

TRAINING TIP If you are in doubt about your fitness level, start with low-level aerobic activities for short periods of time. As you feel ready, try doing longer workouts and activities as suggested in chapter 13.

Testing Your Aerobic Fitness

This is your entrance exam into a structured training program—a test where you actually get out and see how well your body is functioning. Because much of the training for cross-country skiing is done in the spring, summer, and fall, I use a standard walking/running test to evalu-ate general cardiovascular fitness. This test is also used by many elite cross-country skiers to monitor the effectiveness of their training.

Dr. Brian Sharkey, one of the first sports medicine directors for the U.S. Cross-Country Ski Team, developed a 1.5-mile walk/run test you can use to estimate your aerobic fitness. The results of this test are correlated to laboratory investigations to help estimate how much oxygen your body can take in from the air, transport throughout your body, and use in muscles to aerobically burn food fuels.

Your ability to maximally use oxygen is termed your *maximal ven-tilation of oxygen* ($\dot{V}O_2$max). The amount of oxygen that you can use in a given time is a good indicator of your ability to perform endurance activities. To standardize $\dot{V}O_2$max among individuals, scientists express it in terms of milliliters of oxygen burned each minute for each kilogram of body weight (ml/kg/min). At rest, most people will use about 3.5 ml/kg/min. Many well-trained aerobic athletes may have a $\dot{V}O_2$max of over 60 ml/kg/min, with the top values recorded at 90-plus ml/kg/min. This means that our system can increase the amount of oxygen that you use by more than 17 times! The higher your $\dot{V}O_2$max, the faster you should be able to cover a mile or more. Of course, performance is also determined by other factors such as motivation, efficiency of movement, strength, body build, and the percentage of $\dot{V}O_2$max you are able to use for an extended event.

1.5-MILE TEST

1. Use a local school or fitness center track or an accurately measured 1.5-mile stretch of road. Note that the standard running track is a quarter mile, so you would do six laps. Some tracks are shorter, especially indoor tracks, so check in advance and know how many laps you need to do.

2. Start the test at a pace that you can maintain for the entire mile and a half.

3. Increase the pace slightly, if you can, during the final half mile (the last two laps on a standard track).

4. Aim to feel tired but not exhausted at the finish. Within a few minutes, you should feel recovered.

© Terry Wild Studio

The 1.5-mile running test is an excellent method to evaluate your aerobic fitness. Results from this test are well-validated by laboratory methods.

(continued)

5. Look forward with excitement to repeating this test in the future. You can do this test three or four times a year to help evaluate your training performance.

Corrections to your time:

Altitude: For every 1,000 feet in altitude over 2,000 feet, reduce your time by 10 seconds.

Age: To find your age-adjusted relative fitness (not $\dot{V}O_2max$), subtract six seconds from your time for every year over 25.

The faster you run the test, the greater your predicted oxygen uptake will be. The results place you into one of the categories shown in table 3.1.

Table 3.1
1.5-Mile Test Results

Time	Estimated $\dot{V}O_2max$ (ml/kg/min)	Female	Male
6:00	80		World class
7:00	70	World class	Elite
8:00	63	Elite	Excellent
9:00	57	Excellent	Very high
10:00	52	Very high	High
11:00	47	High	Above average
12:00	43	Above average	Average
13:00	38	Average	Below average
14:00	34	Below average	Below average
15:00	29	Below average	Below average

Note. (1) $\dot{V}O_2max$ (ml/kg/min) values for females are generally about 15 percent to 20 percent lower than men. (2) As we age, we lose about 1 ml/kg/min each year after age 25.

Your results will give you a realistic estimate of your beginning fitness and will help you determine where to start with the workouts in part II and the sample programs in part III. Your score reflects only where you are right now, so don't be discouraged if your score is below average. You have adequate fitness for easy ski touring and will find that an aerobic exercise program will be very rewarding. A below average score means you have more room for improvement than people who score higher, and it also means you probably will see bigger gains in subsequent tests. Also note that $\dot{V}O_2$max (ml/kg/min) scores are adjusted for body weight. If you are overweight, reducing your weight will greatly increase your aerobic fitness because you'll have less body mass to move and more aerobic energy to do it with. A training program that begins to use up some of your fat reserves will get you in better shape and also reduce your weight. Your aerobic fitness will get a twofold improvement!

The next chapter will give you some basic instruction in cross-country skiing and the training methods that I use.

Skiing the Right Way

Cross-country skiing and the training that goes with it offer a great variety of activities. You can make training as diverse as you desire, or as simple as using one or two other activities during the months with no snow. In this book, I refer to the nonskiing activities as *dryland training*. Like many others, you may find that the varied training for cross-country skiing is as enjoyable as cross-country skiing itself, and you will grow to love the versatility that comes with learning new activities.

This chapter presents a short overview of the techniques of cross-country skiing as well as basic information about the most popular dryland activities. The detailed subject of technique for cross-country skiing is beyond the scope of this book, but there are many fine books and videos available on cross-country skiing, racing, touring, and backcountry skiing to guide you in developing your skiing efficiency. Ultimately, you will find that improvements in technique go hand in hand with improvements in strength and endurance.

Cross-Country Ski Techniques

Cross-country ski technique can be divided into two major categories: classic technique and skating technique. Within each of these two broad categories there are many different techniques and skills to learn.

Classic techniques, in general, are those in which the skis are kept moving straight forward in the direction of travel (except when turning). The ski bases have either special kick wax applied to the base or a no-wax pattern carved into the ski base that allows the ski to glide forward but not to slip backward when the skier pushes against the ski using proper technique. On prepared trails, classic skiing uses two tracks, or grooves, that are molded into the snow by special grooming machines. Classic skiing also includes backcountry skiing with heavier skis to handle the rugged terrain, loose snow, and steeper climbs.

Skating technique is the newcomer to the sport of cross-country skiing and is very popular with racers. Ski skating requires a well-packed track or a hard snow surface. The motions are very similar to in-line skating or speed skating on ice, with the addition of poling with both arms together. Skating skis do not have kick wax or no-wax patterns on the ski bases because the skis are always gliding, even when the skier pushes off. Ski skating requires a higher level of fitness to perform at a minimal speed than does the classic technique, which can be done from a slow walk on skis to fast racing technique.

Of course, unless you are skiing in a regulated race, you may use either skate or classic techniques at any time. It is possible to skate on waxable classic skis, even with kick wax on the skis, but most skiers will use separate, special equipment for the two different techniques.

Efficiency in cross-country skiing requires arm power and arm endurance to be high enough to allow for effective pushes with the poles. After the initial learning stages, when the poles are used for balance, the poles in cross-country skiing are used to help maintain the glide of the skis. The skier with good technique uses the major muscles of both arms and legs. The photos that follow give examples of the different techniques in cross-country skiing. Each of these techniques has many variations and individual styles.

Diagonal Technique

Diagonal technique is what most people think of when cross-country skiing is mentioned. Skiers glide over the snow using alternating legs and arms. The faster you go, the more extended your arms and legs become and the more your body leans forward.

© Dennis G. Hendricks

Diagonal technique—classic skiing.

Double Pole Technique

Double poling can be done in classic or skating technique. Skis are facing the direction of travel down the track. All of the energy for forward motion is generated from the arms and torso. The poles angle close to the snow during much of the pole push.

© Dennis G. Hendricks

Double pole technique—classic or skating technique.

Kick-double pole—classic technique.

© Dennis G. Hendricks

Kick-Double Pole Technique

This is a classic technique. It is just like the double pole, but you add a kick or a push with one leg. The forward arm swings forward as the leg kicks, then you plant the poles in the snow to initiate the pole push.

Downhill techniques.

© Dennis G. Hendricks

Downhill Techniques

If you lower your body position into a tuck, you'll be more aerodynamic and you'll go faster. Keep your weight square over the center of your feet and relax to stay balanced. Start with the position in the photo, and as you get more comfortable with speed you can move to the lower positions.

TRAINING TIP To learn to handle more challenging downhills, start by only descending the bottom part of a hill. Find a downhill that intimidates you. Climb up just a little way, then glide down. Climb back up again, a little higher this time. Glide down again. Keep repeating, climbing up and gliding down, a little higher each time, but stay within your comfort zone. You will gradually become more proficient on the downhills, and you'll get a good workout in the process.

V1 Skating Technique

V1 skating technique is also called *offset skating*. On every second leg push, use the poles in a double poling motion starting the poling push at the same moment that you set the ski on that side down. Note the flexion of the upper body and pole positions.

© Dennis G. Hendricks

V1 skating technique.

V2 and V2 alternate skating techniques.

V2 Skating Technique

V2 skating technique is also called *one-step*, and it requires good balance. It has alternating double pole pushes sequenced between pushes with the right and left legs. To get the rhythm, keep repeating this chant: "pole (with both poles), push (right leg), pole (both arms), push (left leg)." The timing between pole plants and leg pushes is about equal.

© Dennis G. Hendricks

V2 Alternate Skating Technique

V2 alternate skating technique is also called *two-step*. It's like V2 skating technique, but poling is done on only one side. This flowing, rhythmic technique is popular among high-level racers, but it requires good physical fitness and leg and upper-body strength. The rhythm is "pole (with both poles), step (one leg), step (other leg), pole, step, step," and keep repeating.

Techniques for Dryland Training Activities

People have their own preferences concerning the activities and training they do when not skiing. A short list of possible activities, approximately ranked according to the time high-level skiers spend on an activity, appears in table 4.1. The table also lists how average skiers might spend their training.

Table 4.1
Average Amounts of Training Time Spent in Different Activities by High-Level Racers and Average Skiers During the Winter and Dryland Periods of the Year

Activity	Winter All skiers	Dryland High-level skier	Dryland Average skier
Cross-country skiing	78%	5%	0%
Roller skiing (or in-line skating with poles)	0%	20%	0-20%
Running and jogging (without poles)	7%	15%	15-20%
Cycling	0%	10%	5-20%
Hiking or walking with poles	0%	15%	10-15%
Strength training			
Hill bounding	0%	3%	2-3%
Roller board	0%	2%	3-5%
Plyometrics	3%	4%	0-3%
Weight training	2%	6%	4-5%
Swimming	5%	10%	0-20%
Other sports (soccer, gymnastics, basketball, etc.)	5%	10%	5-15%

All cross-country skiers need to spend time running, jogging, and hiking with poles. Arm fitness is a critical component of cross-country skiing, and skiers need to spend time training the major muscles of their arms for both strength and endurance.

Specificity of training is a basic fitness principle. Cross-country skiers can ski only when there is snow, however. The most specific summer activity is training on roller skis. Roller skis are essential for high-level racers, but most of the rest of us compromise on specific training during the summer and elect to do a wide variety of sports and activities. The net result is that you may not ski quite as fast, but you'll be a well-rounded athlete with a better chance of avoiding overuse and imbalance problems that can happen when you overtrain some muscles and neglect others.

Running and Jogging

Skiers spend a lot of time running or jogging, so it is important to learn a few fundamentals. Run quietly. If you can hear yourself "pounding the pavement," learn to run with a shorter stride and to absorb more of the shock with your knees. Use your whole foot during running. Land with your knees slightly bent so that they can absorb the shock. Think of running as prancing, quiet and lively.

Let your arms swing in rhythm with your legs as you run. Feel your hands relax, and release the tension throughout your body. Keep your elbows bent and pump your arms to maintain a good running rhythm. Finally, keep your shoulders relaxed and don't let the deltoid muscles work during the arm swing. Relaxed shoulders and arms are also necessary for good ski technique. The shoulders and trunk should have minimal rotational movement.

If you experience foot or knee pain while running, get professional advice from a podiatrist. A running coach might be able to help you with your technique.

Most of the running that skiers will do can be very relaxed. It's better to run on hills than on flats. Slow down on the uphills, even to a brisk walk if necessary. The lifting that comes with running uphill trains the muscles for skiing more specifically than running on flat ground does.

Cycling

Cycling is a great activity for skiers fresh off of the ski season when their legs are not used to the pounding of running. Easy cycling also offers a great recovery workout between harder days of training. Of course, cycling can be a very strenuous workout in itself. Based on the principle of specificity, it makes sense to do your longer and higher-intensity workouts using activities that are as specific to skiing as possible. Road cycling, because it's not highly specific in muscle function to cross-country skiing, is thus better used for recovery and very easy workouts.

If you like to bike but also want to get the most cross-country skiing benefit, consider biking in hilly terrain. You could also go mountain biking on hilly trails for a harder workout. Standing up on the pedals is good ski training, and the interval nature of mountain biking is similar to the demands in cross-country skiing where there are periods of hard uphill work followed by periods of downhill glide and rest.

Be sure that your bike is properly fitted for your body and that the seat is high enough so that your knee is just slightly bent when the pedal is at the low point of its revolution. If you don't know how to properly adjust your bike to fit, stop by a local bike shop. They will be able to quickly get you on your way. A properly adjusted bike will help you avoid injury and will make your riding more enjoyable.

Hiking and Walking With Poles

If you don't do endurance training for your arms during the dryland season, they will be your weak link during the winter. Arm strength is important not only for skiing, but also for your long-term health and independence into old age. Lack of arm strength is one of the major factors that force elderly people to seek help for their daily living. Unfortunately, we live in a society where very few people use their arms during daily work.

Hiking and walking with poles is exactly what it sounds like. To do this activity well, it helps to have shorter poles than you use for cross-country skiing. An inexpensive pair of poles will serve you well. The poles should be about 70 to 75 percent of your height. Skiers usually alternate their arms so that the pole in the hand opposite the foot that is stepping forward is planted at the same time that the foot lands. The pole should be planted to angle toward the rear. Walk briskly, using long steps and pushing comfortably on your poles, for the duration of the session. Pole hiking is trail walking in hills, contrasted with pole walking, which tends to be on gentler trails.

Pole walking on pavement may eventually cause elbow pain or stress, so you should walk on dirt or grass trails. The more conscious you are about using your poles in training, the better you will be able to use your arms during skiing.

Roller Skiing or In-Line Skating With Poles

If you choose to train on roller skis, it is enjoyable to hook up with other skiers in your area who know the safe routes and best areas. There is a good chance that there are already individuals or groups in your area who get out regularly.

When roller skiing, the first concern is for safety. Here are a few rules:

- Purchase good quality roller skis.
- Purchase carbide tips for your poles and keep them sharpened. (Many good cross-country poles come with winter tips that are carbide.)
- Always wear a helmet.
- Know your route and avoid steep downhills, gravel, railroad tracks, and other hazards.

- Do not roller ski on busy roads; instead, use bike paths and quiet roads with wide shoulders.
- Wear light gloves in case you fall. Knee and elbow pads are a good idea.
- Check your roller skis before use for loose screws. Tighten all nuts frequently.
- If sharing the road with traffic, wear a reflective, high-visibility vest.

Many athletes use roller skis for technique work and to refine specific techniques—there are good models for both skating and classic technique. The drawback of roller skis is that they are quite expensive and require a fair deal of skiing skill before one should venture out on them. In addition, skiers can develop many bad technique habits on roller skis. The most practical use of roller skis is to use them for long, double pole workouts, thus maximizing the training effect for the arms. Use running for leg training to complement double poling on roller skis. If you focus on double poling while roller skiing, you will find your arm endurance and power quickly increasing.

© Photo Network/Eric Sanford

In-line skates are great training for cross-country skiing during the summer. Roller ski models are available for classic skiing or skating. Some combination models work adequately for both techniques.

In-line skates are a great alternative to roller skis. In-line skates tend to be much faster than roller skis and so do not give as much resistance for training. However, in-line skates still provide a great training tool. You can work out with or without poles. When using poles while in-line skating, skating techniques or double poling works well. In order to give your arms a better workout, try long, double pole workouts. Use your skates on a path with gentle hills to add resistance to an easy workout. I outline several in-line skate workouts in part II.

Strength Training

Cross-country skiers use many methods for strength training. The range of strength training goals runs from increasing specific endurance to building greater maximal strength for individual muscles. The methods include weight training and plyometric bounding exercises, specific strength exercises such as hill bounding and roller board training, and power endurance exercises such as uphill double poling on roller skis or in-line skates.

Weight Training and Plyometrics. Specifics about weight training and plyometrics (explosive bounding exercises) are beyond the scope of this book, but both can be very beneficial to your skiing. For more information, refer to a good text or talk with a professional strength trainer.

Hill Bounding. This is bounding up a hill using your arms and legs in a coordinated effort. Alternate the poles and arms with the legs as you bound up a moderately steep hill. The object is to use long bounds during which both feet are off the ground at the same time.

Arm Training With a Roller Board. A roller board is an inclined ramp with a wheeled platform that the skier can kneel on. Two ropes attached to the top of the ramp and act as "poles" with which skiers pull themselves up and lower themselves down the ramp. The resistance is controlled by increasing or decreasing the angle of the ramp. This is a great arm training device that you can manufacture easily at home. Most serious skiers have a roller board in their basement or in their backyard.

Putting together a good training program for cross-country skiing means juggling a lot of information. I will help you throughout the book to understand the concepts and how they relate to each other. Now it is time to get warmed up.

Hill bounding with poles. Notice the time when both feet are off the ground.

Using a roller board is very specific arm work for cross-country skiing.

5

Warming Up and Cooling Down

Sport requires dynamic movements, which in turn require a flexible range of motion. Cross-country skiing is no exception. One of the beauties of cross-country skiing is that it is easy on the body, having few movements that pound or jar joints. Cross-country skiing causes few acute injuries, but athletes who, before training or skiing, neglect to warm up with easy exercise and stretching may experience nagging overuse injuries. Any sport with repetitive movements will put strains on joints, tendons, ligaments, and muscles that are frequently used and improperly trained or warm before they are used. Cross-country skiing performed in a cold environment compounds the need for a gradual warm-up of the deep muscles before strenuous exercise. I find that as I age it takes longer every year to be fully warmed up for intense exercise and I may need to ski as much as five kilometers, gradually increasing the pace, before I feel ready to work hard.

TRAINING TIP The more intense the workout, the longer you need to warm up. My general rule of thumb is to warm up 6-8 minutes for easy workouts, 10-15 minutes for medium-intensity workouts, and 15-25 minutes for high-intensity workouts.

Inactive muscles are not ready to perform strenuous activity. Many injuries happen in sports where participants perform brief bursts of activity after inactive periods. The classic example is in softball or baseball, where batters sprint to first base after sitting on the bench. They are asking their muscles to perform in an all-out task without being gradually warmed up.

The term *warm-up* has been used to mean different things. In a strict sense, it simply means starting out any activity with very light exercise and gradually increasing the intensity as the muscles become more flexible and warm. One of the by-products of a working muscle is a small amount of heat. The circulation system removes the heat, but it also slightly raises the internal temperature of the working muscles. This warming of the muscles allows for better oxygen diffusion and greater flexibility, and it speeds up the oxidation of fuels for more efficient use of your muscles.

A good warm-up will make your exercise session more enjoyable, help prevent injury, improve the training gains, and make training feel easier. Muscles do not like to go suddenly from inactivity to high intensity. A smooth increase in intensity over a period of time will make the adjustment easier.

Finding the Appropriate Warm-Up for You

Every individual has specific warm-up needs that may change daily. Your training of the prior day or days, your age, genetics, the activity that you'll be performing, time of day, external temperature, health, and other factors such as your daily work schedule all affect the kind of warm-up you need. Learn how to listen to your body and understand its signals.

The general concept of a warm-up is to begin your chosen activity for the training session at a very low intensity, which keeps your heart rate below 50 percent of your maximal heart rate (which I will discuss in part II). For cross-country skiing, this means moving very slowly without uphills. Over a period of 5 to 15 minutes, you will gradually increase the level of your exercise until you reach the intensity planned for the workout. The higher the intensity of the planned workout, the longer the warm-up will take. Cross-country skiers who are racing in a short 5K race will often ski the entire course before the race, skiing the first half very slowly and then increasing their speed until they are at, or near, race speed for the last two to three minutes. They will also try to time their warm-up so that they arrive back at the start only a few minutes before their start time. If warm-ups are so important for high-level athletes who spend lots of time stretching and are able to ski a great deal, think about how much more important warming up is for the rest of us who get out less often and are not as well trained. As we age, we also take longer to warm up. Many of the master skiers with whom I work will warm up gradually for as much as 30 minutes before doing any strenuous activity. Keep in mind that these are well-trained skiers who average 7 to 10 hours a week of training.

To judge your warm-up needs, pay attention to how you feel when you start a workout. You'll probably feel a little tired as your body begins to get going. After several minutes, you should begin to feel a little loosened up and relaxed. As you increase your intensity, you will begin to feel warm and will become more energized. Be sure not to increase your effort until it feels easy to do so. Pay attention to how you are feeling. If you train with a group, encourage everyone to keep the pace down until everyone feels ready for the planned workout.

Your warm-up is also a time to evaluate pretraining tiredness and your will and ability to train that day. Getting started is always the most difficult part of training. Many mornings you might feel tired and might prematurely decide not to go out for your exercise. However, if you take the step out the door and go through a good warm-up you may find yourself feeling great. Of course, you may finish a warm-up and know that it is time to head in for the day if you still feel very tired. Don't make decisions not to train until after your warm-up.

You can also evaluate aches and pains during your warm-up. If you felt a minor pain during your training the day before, a warm-up will help you properly evaluate your condition. As you warm up, the stiffness and pain might disappear and you'll feel great. If the pain signals an injury that is going to need some time, you will also know that during the warm-up. If joint or muscle pain increases as you are warming up, you should take the day off. If you think the injury might require some time to heal, get professional help early so you miss as little training time as possible.

The bottom line: Do a gradual warm-up and believe what your body is telling you. You will know if it is time to move on or to slow down.

Cooling Down and Stretching Out

Just as it is important to warm up and get your muscles ready for exercise, it is important at the end of exercise to slowly reduce the intensity and allow your muscles and circulation to slow down to near resting.

When you finish skiing or training, your heart may be pumping hard, your body is hot, and most of your blood is circulating to the working muscles. If you come to an abrupt stop, your working muscles will no longer be assisting the venous return of blood to your heart and a great deal of blood may pool in your legs and arms and leave little to circulate to your brain and other organs. You might become light-headed or even pass out. The cure? Do a cool-down of easy skiing until your heart has slowed down and your temperature is near normal.

The worst thing you can do is to finish a hard ski or other training activity and then jump in your car and drive home. Don't sit down right after strenuous work. Continue with light activity, keeping your muscles moving for 5 to 10 minutes.

At the end of a workout, winter or summer, your clothing may be damp or wet with sweat. You may become quite chilled. Be sure to have a dry set of clothing along, or at least a dry shirt, and change right after your cool-down.

The final activity before ending the workout is to stretch. Cross-country skiing, like all training activities, will cause exercised muscles to tighten. Running and pounding activities or strength training results in especially tight muscles. Running and skiing tend to cause the hamstring and calf muscles to tighten up. Skiing also tightens your back and often the anterior tibialis (shin muscle). It is very important to stretch while your muscles are still a little warm from the activity, but before you completely cool off and begin to get stiff.

I suggest stretching after exercise. My experience is that winter athletes don't like to warm up and then stop in the cold, or go back into a building to stretch. Postexercise stretching works well in practical terms, whether you stretch in the chalet or as soon as you get home. Stretching after exercise will lengthen the tight muscles and leave you feeling loose and relaxed. If you stretch while your muscles are still warm, there is the least chance of injury. If you do have to wait awhile to find a suitable place to stretch, be sure to start your stretching slowly.

Daily stretching will benefit you by increasing the range of motion your joints can move through without resistance, reducing acute and overtraining injuries, and improving coordination and rhythm in all of your sport activities. Stretching is important for everyone, but vital for master athletes. As we age, especially after age 30, we begin to lose range of motion unless we make a concerted effort to maintain flexibility. Follow these rules as you stretch:

1. Get used to stretching with gradual increases in tension, and then hold (static stretching) for 10 to 20 seconds after you feel you have reached the limit of your flexibility. When you are at a proper tension, you should feel a slight discomfort but not pain.
2. After several weeks of good static stretching, you can incorporate *very gentle* bounces into your stretches after you have done two or three static holds of each stretch. Reaching for a slightly greater stretch should not be painful, and it needs to be done gently. You should bounce only slightly beyond the stretch that you are reaching with the static stretches.
3. Avoid weight-bearing stretches such as toe touches with your legs straight. It is better to do hamstring stretches separate from lower back stretches.
4. Unless you are working with a qualified professional, do not use weights or partners to provide additional stretch.
5. Your goal should be to increase your flexibility to a range of motion that is greater than what is necessary for your activities. Remember that stretching is not a competitive sport, but rather a personal activity to gently improve your own range of motion.

On the following pages are 10 beneficial stretches for cross-country skiing. These stretches focus on the major muscles used in cross-country skiing, but will also benefit you following cycling and running. If you find specific muscles that are still tight after this set of stretches, use additional stretches to work them. There are many good books on stretching to help you with some of the more difficult muscles.

Winter is often an inhospitable environment for stretching, especially after you are warmed up and sweating a little or when you've just finished a workout and are ready to get in out of the cold. I selected the first four stretches, those for the hamstrings (rear thigh), quadriceps (front thigh), and upper and lower calves, so you can do them in a standing position with only a wall and a table or railing. Stretching these muscles is critical for effective skiing.

Hamstrings

© Dennis G. Hendricks

Immediately following your cool-down (this one is also great just after a warm-up), find a railing or picnic table about waist high or lower. Swing one leg forward up on the railing and then slowly reach forward toward your toe. If possible, hold your foot and pull forward gently. If you can't reach your foot, lean forward. Grab your ankle and pull forward gently. Focus on trying to bring your belly button toward your toe. Hold for 10 to 20 seconds, relax, and switch legs. Repeat two or three times with each leg. This is a great stretch that is easy on your back. Tight hamstrings are the primary cause of low back pain in cross-country skiers.

Quadriceps

© Dennis G. Hendricks

Stand on one leg. It helps to have a wall for balance. Bend one leg behind you and grasp your forefoot with the hand on the same side. Keep your stance leg slightly bent and pull your opposite heel toward your buttocks. Take care not to over-compress your knee. Repeat this stretch on the other side. Avoid this stretch if it hurts your knees.

Lower Calf

© Dennis G. Hendricks

Face a wall with your feet about two to three feet away from it. Using the wall for balance, lift one leg. Keeping the heel of your other foot on the ground, bend the knee of your stance leg forward and toward the ground. Hold for 10 to 20 seconds and switch legs. Repeat a couple of times on each leg. This should stretch the lower and deeper soleus muscle of your calf and thereby improve flexibility in your ankle when your knee is bent, which is critical to good technique in cross-country skiing.

Upper Calf

© Dennis G. Hendricks

Move farther from the wall and stand on one leg with the other leg draped behind the front leg. With a straight knee on the stance leg, and the heel on the ground, try to move your hips gently towards the ground so that the angle of the leg to the ground is decreased and you feel a stretch in the upper calf. Like the previous stretch, this stretch will improve flexibility in your ankles.

Buttocks and Hip

© Dennis G. Hendricks

In skating, you use the leg abductors while pushing to the outside. If you skate a lot, this stretch will help. Indoors, sitting on a floor, extend your legs in front of you. Bend your left leg and cross it over your right and place your left foot flat on the floor right beside your right knee. Leaning on your left arm for balance, use your right elbow to push on the outside of your left knee as you twist your entire body to the left. Try to look backward over your left shoulder. Repeat on the other side.

Lower Back

© Dennis G. Hendricks

Do this stretch slowly. Kneel on hands and knees and start by reaching your left arm forward horizontally and your right leg horizontally to the rear. Stretch both your arm and leg out as far as you can reach without arching your back or lifting your hand or foot above the level of your back. Hold for two to three seconds and then repeat with the opposite arm and leg. Repeat this cycle three or four times very slowly with control.

Triceps

© Dennis G. Hendricks

Triceps, the upper-arm muscles that extend your elbow, get a major workout during poling and may get quite stiff. Stand with your right arm overhead, then reach with the right hand down the middle of your back as far as you can reach. If possible, use your left hand to reach up behind your back and help to gently pull the right hand down. If you can't grasp hands behind your back, use your left hand to push the elbow gently down from the top. Hold for 10 to 20 seconds. Repeat twice on both sides.

Leg Adductors

© Dennis G. Hendricks

Skating requires lots of lateral movements with the legs. The leg adductor muscles are likely to get tight. Sit on the floor with your knees bent at about 90 degrees or more and the soles of your feet together. Grasp your ankles and use your elbows to apply gentle pressure to push your knees outward and toward the ground. Keep your back straight and breathing relaxed. Hold for 15 to 20 seconds. Repeat two or three times.

Abdominals

© Dennis G. Hendricks

Lie in a prone position and place your palms flat on the ground by your shoulders. Slowly use your arms to raise your torso up. Focus on leaving your belly button close to the floor. Raise yourself up only as far as you feel comfortable, and then try to further relax and let your stomach sag toward the floor. Breathe out as you let the tension go. Hold for 10 to 20 seconds, lower yourself, relax, and then repeat two to four times.

Neck

© Dennis G. Hendricks

Start with a gentle rotation of your neck to get the kinks out. Now reach both hands behind your back. Grasp your left elbow with your right hand. While keeping your torso straight pull the left elbow gently behind your back and bend your head towards the right. You should feel a good stretch on the left side of your neck. Repeat two or three times on each side.

We have come a long way together and it is time to get ready to begin your workouts. In the next section, I introduce you to the workout zones, describing how to use them and how to follow the plans that I've put together to lead you to optimal fitness.

PART II

CROSS-COUNTRY SKIING WORKOUT ZONES

Training is the process of slowly increasing the demands on your muscles and aerobic system to elicit a training response. You need to first build an aerobic base with long, easy training of increasing volume, then add higher-intensity training and finally speed training.

To develop a simple but effective method to bring training together into an understandable routine, this book uses a series of color-coded workouts based on heart rate and intensity. Workouts in each zone fall into a range of intensity (low, medium, high). Green training is the easiest, followed by Blue, Purple, Yellow, Orange, and finally Red, the most difficult.

Each workout has a suggested duration. Thirty minutes for the main body of the workout is the dividing point between the short workouts and the long workouts.

WORKOUT COLOR ZONES			
Zone (chapter)	Type of workout	Intensity (RPE/%maxHR)	Time
Green (6)	Low intensity, short duration	2–4/60–74	<30 min
Blue (7)	Low intensity, long duration	2–4/60–74	>30 min
Purple (8)	Medium intensity, short duration	5–7/75–89	<30 min
Yellow (9)	Medium intensity, long duration	5–7/75–89	>30 min
Orange (10)	High intensity, short duration	7–10/85–100	<30 min
Red (11)	High intensity, long duration	7–8/85–94	>30 min

Within each zone, the workouts progress in difficulty, with the early workouts being the easiest and the final workouts of each zone being the hardest. Each workout has a winter option (usually skiing) and a summer option. Many of the cross-country skiing workouts can also be done on one of the better cross-country ski simulators, such as the Nordictrak® XC exerciser. You can always substitute your own mode of exercise, but pay close attention to the duration and intensity.

Each workout contains all the information you need to perform the workout—a description, duration (including the activity portion and total time with warm-up and cool-down), distance, effort, warm-up and cool-down, calories burned, and comments. A few more words about some of the workout features.

Intensity

Learning how to evaluate how hard you are working during a workout is critical to any successful training program. You must learn to listen to your body and be truthful in your evaluation of the intensity. Training at too high an intensity is the most common error in sports and leads to overtraining, injury, staleness, and poor long-term results. Much of the training suggested in this book will be easier than you may currently associate with the concept of training. Many famous coaches have often reminded their athletes of a basic training axiom: "Train slow to race fast." Of course, sometimes you have to push the limits and challenge your body. I won't forget to let you sweat now and then.

I give you three ways to check your training intensity in the workouts: your heart rate as a percentage of your estimated maximum heart rate (% max HR), and two subjective ratings. The first subjective rating is the Rating of Perceived Exertion (RPE) scale developed by Dr. Gunnar Borg. The second scale is one I use all the time with master and junior athletes, which I call the *talk scale*. An estimate of intensity using all three scales is noted in most workouts. Refer to table II.1 to see how these three scales match up with one another. What scale you use is not important; the goal is to get some idea of how hard you're working as you do the workouts.

Using Percentage of Maximum Heart Rate

There is a good linear relationship between heart rate (HR) and work intensity for each individual. However, there is no close correlation between HR, age, training status, sex, or race other than a broad formula that may be off quite a lot for any given person. However, HR works well to get you into approximate training zones, and over time you will develop a good feeling for the appropriate HRs for your training. Being familiar with HR zones is especially helpful when you change activities and try new exercises for which you do not have a good perception, especially when you start using both arms and legs.

Table II.1
Rating Your Level of Exercise Intensity

Heart rate % of max HR	Perception of effort	Borg RPE	Talk scale
<60%	Minimum intensity	1	Singing (full songs)
60–69%	Low intensity	2–3	Talking (telling stories)
70–74%	Low to medium intensity	4	Talking (sentences)
75–84%	Medium intensity	5–6	Clear thinking (limited talking)
85–89%	Medium to high intensity	7	Focus only on task of training
90–99%	High intensity	8–9	Working very hard
>99%	Maximal intensity	10	Not going to last long

Heart rate zones may also change from activity to activity, but don't worry about that for now.

The easiest way to determine an estimated maximal heart rate is to use these formulas:

Men: Max HR = 220 – age
Women: Max HR = 226 – age

If you are a 36-year-old woman, your max HR would be 190 beats per minute:

226 – 36 = 190

Multiply your chosen intensity by this result, for example, if you're planning to do a Blue workout in the 60 to 69 percent of max range:

190 (max HR) x 60% (lower end of range) = 114
190 (max HR) x 69% (upper end of range) = 131

Therefore, your target heart rate range is 114 to 131 beats per minute.

Using the RPE scale

If you can be honest with yourself, the RPE scale might be the easiest scale for you to use. It has been extensively researched and well documented to correlate well with objective measurements of exertion, such as heart rate.

A general rule of thumb is that activities that you think you could maintain for about 30 minutes before complete exhaustion (such as a 30-minute ski race) will be about RPE 6 to 7, and an activity that you could maintain for an hour would probably be closer to RPE 5. A fast walk might be an RPE 2 to 3, but it all depend on your fitness.

Using the Talk Scale

This scale has five levels; *singing, talking, clear thinking, focusing,* and *barely hangin' on.* The titles refer to how you feel and what activity you are able to do while exercising.

- **Singing.** Very easy exercise. At this level of activity you could sing whole songs and not be short of breath.
- **Talking.** Low- to medium-intensity exercise. Here you can talk to your training partners in full sentences, though you may occasionally have to catch your breath. If you find it difficult to keep up a conversation, you are in the next intensity level and going too hard for talking intensity.
- **Clear thinking.** Medium exercise. This is a comfortable level to train for most people. You are working a bit harder than a level that would allow easy talking, but your brain has plenty of

oxygen and you can become lost in your own world of thought and mull over lots of creative ideas. The exercise just kind of takes care of itself. This is about the intensity of a marathon for most master, non-elite runners.

- **Focusing.** You are now working hard enough so that you need to focus on the task of the exercise to keep yourself working at this intensity. Your breathing will be harder, you cannot talk with those around you, and you may be sweating. This is generally the intensity for medium-distance races.
- **Barely hangin' on.** At this intensity you can go for only a couple of minutes or less. I jokingly call it "brain dead." Time spent at this intensity is always very short, generally less than 20 seconds in an interval format, with long rest periods.

Each of the three intensity scales has its strengths and weaknesses. As you train, your heart rate will change and the percentage of maximal HR that corresponds to your subjective ratings for each RPE will also change. How you rate your effort on the RPE scale will also depend on your interpretation of easy, medium, and hard.

Total Calories Burned

This will give you an idea of the total energy that you will expend during the workout. This number is related to the overall difficulty, but some of the long-distance, low-intensity workouts will burn more calories even though they're lower in total difficulty.

I recommend many different types of activities for training, thus the energy cost, measured in calories, may vary widely from workout to workout or depending on the exercise format that you actually decide to use. Cross-country skiing, because it uses more muscles than nearly any other sport, burns more calories per minute at a given intensity than most other sports. The number of calories that you burn per mile will also depend greatly on your technique, the number of hills, your weight, and other factors.

I put together a simple table to give you an idea of the caloric cost for sample workouts based on intensity and type of activity (see table II.2). The actual measure of work is the kilocalorie (kcal). These are the same calories that are listed on all of the foods that you eat. To figure total cost in kcal, multiply the length of your training time (minutes) in a zone and then adjust for your body weight.

Each workout also gives an estimated number of kcal burned. The calories given in the workouts and in table II.2 are based on a 150-pound person, so you need to add or subtract 10 percent for each 15 pounds above or below 150. For example, if a workout lists that it will cost about 500 kcal, and you weigh 165 pounds, your cost would

Table II.2
Caloric Cost of Cross-Country Skiing and Other Activities

| | Kcal/min | | | | |
Zone	Cross-country skiing	Running	Cycling	Ski simulator	Swimming
Green and Blue	12	10	9	11	9
Purple and Yellow	18	15	13	17	15
Orange and Red	23	20	17	21	21

To figure total cost in kcal, multiply the length of your training time (minutes) in a zone and then adjust for your body weight.

be 10 percent greater, or 500 kcal + 50 kcal = 550 kcal. A person who weighs 120 pounds would need to reduce the listed caloric cost by 20 percent, or 500 kcal – 100 kcal = 400 kcal.

Distance

Distances in the workouts are listed as kilometers. Nearly all ski trails now use the standard kilometer distance markings, but there are still some trail systems using mile markers. You might need to convert distances from miles to kilometers so that you can keep your records in a standard format. Table II.3 will help you convert between kilometers and miles. There are 1.61 kilometers per mile.

You now should have an idea of where you want to start with your training. After you scan through the workouts in chapters 6 through 11 and read chapter 12 to design your own program, you won't have much more to do before you put on your training clothes and head out the door.

Table II.3
Converting Miles to Kilometers

Miles	Kilometers
0.3	0.5
0.6	1
1.2	2
1.9	3
2.5	4
3.1	5
3.7	6
4.3	7
5.0	8
5.6	9
6.2	10
9.3	15
12.4	20
15.5	25
18.6	30
24.9	40
31.1	50

6

Green Zone

The Green zone is one of the most important tools for a new program, for recovery, and for integrating new training types and modes into your program. You should be able to talk in full sentences while training in this zone, and your heart rate should be below 74 percent of maximum. The Green zone workouts are less than 30 minutes long.

If you are just beginning your training program, or if you are adding a new type of training activity (such as running), Green zone workouts will allow you to gradually get your muscles ready for more intense activities. If you're already aerobically fit, Green zone training will help you recover more quickly between days with longer or harder workouts. Over the past 20 years, almost every successful athlete in aerobic events has heard the saying "Go slow to race fast," yet going easy in training is still one of the most elusive goals of athletes. For those days when you just don't feel up to longer training or you've had a stressful day, the Green zone will be just the ticket for relieving stress and gaining the relaxing benefits of easy exercise.

In the Green zone you will be introduced to several concepts:

- **Easy training.** No matter what the activity, you should be able to talk freely, without shortness of breath, while training in the Green zone. You may not feel like you're working hard enough to call the activity training, and you probably won't sweat unless it's a warm day. You should find these activities to be relaxing, restful, and refreshing. Your heart rate should not exceed about 74 percent of maximum and your RPE should be in the "easy" range.
- **Steady state.** Maintain a steady heart rate throughout the exercise at the suggested RPE.
- **Recovery.** Use light and easy exercise along with stretching to help your body recover from more difficult training.
- **Natural intervals.** Try to forget old notions about interval workouts being gut wrenching. *Interval* simply means a period of higher than normal activity followed by a period of easier activity or rest. The final workout in this section introduces you to easy, natural intervals. For natural intervals, you will ski on trails with some hills so that the terrain naturally brings periods of hard work and easy work. For Green zone workouts, the hills should be gentle. The goal is to keep your speed relatively constant throughout the exercise. When you ski uphill, your heart rate will go up slightly and you will work harder. Your heart rate should drop as you glide down the trail. The major benefit of interval training is that it requires slightly higher than normal intensities for short periods, followed by periods of rest. The intervals provide effective training to build a base for higher-intensity workouts than steady state training brings.

VERY EASY SKIING
TOTAL TIME: 25-35 minutes

WARM-UP: Stretch hamstrings gently, then walk on your skis until you can break into a comfortable rhythm. Slowly, over about 5 minutes, let your HR rise up to 65% of max.

WORKOUT

Winter activity: Classic skiing on level terrain

Summer activity: Brisk walking with some jogging

Exerciser: Ski simulator set at low resistance. Set level to give you an HR of 65% of max.

Distance: 2-3K, but no more

Time: 10-20 minutes

Effort: RPE 2-3; 60-69% max HR. You should be able to talk easily with a training partner.

COOL-DOWN: Slow down during the final 5 minutes until you're walking on your skis. Finish with 5 minutes of stretching.

CALORIES BURNED: 150-200

COMMENTS

Go at an intensity that you know is easy. Depending on the snow conditions and your ability, this may be a walk or a nice gliding tour. Vary your speed a little. When you feel your heart rate going up a little, be sure to back off and slow down again. You can do this workout on a packed trail or touring in the woods. If you can't keep your heart rate down while maintaining a glide, ski for a few minutes then walk on your skis for a few minutes.

2

VERY EASY SKIING
TOTAL TIME: 30-40 minutes

WARM-UP: Start slowly, over about 5 minutes, and let your HR rise up to 65% of max.

WORKOUT

Winter activity: Classic skiing on level terrain

Summer activity: Walking with poles and pushing a little on the poles

Exerciser: Ski simulator set at low resistance. Set level to give you an HR of 65% max.

Distance: 3-4K

Time: 15-25 minutes

Effort: RPE 2-3; 60-69% max HR. You should be able to talk easily with a training partner.

COOL-DOWN: Slow down over the final 5 minutes. Finish with 5 minutes of stretching. Focus on calf muscles, hamstrings, and arms.

CALORIES BURNED: 200-260

COMMENTS

Try to maintain a steady pace. Don't move on to longer workouts until you can maintain a steady pace for the entire distance. Your ability and the snow conditions will determine the speed and distance that you go.

VERY EASY SKIING
TOTAL TIME: 30-45 minutes

3

WARM-UP: Slowly, over about 5 minutes, let your HR rise up to 65% of max.

WORKOUT

Winter activity: Classic skiing on level terrain

Summer activity: Bike riding on flat trails or road

Exerciser: Ski simulator set at low resistance. Set level to give you an HR of 65% of max.

Distance: 3-5K, but no more

Time: 15-30 minutes

Effort: RPE 2-3; 60-69% max HR. You should be able to talk easily with a training partner.

COOL-DOWN: Last 5 minutes reduce the speed and intensity. Finish with 5 minutes of stretching. Try to do the entire set of 10 stretches covered in chapter 5.

CALORIES BURNED: 225-285

COMMENTS

When you can finish this workout without needing to stop for rest, you'll be ready to begin building your aerobic base.

WORKOUT 4

SWIMMING
TOTAL TIME: 20-25 minutes

WARM-UP: Slowly, over about 5 minutes, let your HR rise up to 65% of max.

WORKOUT

Winter activity: Swimming in a 25-meter pool

Summer activity: Swimming in a 25-meter pool

Distance: Do any stroke for 50 meters (two laps), rest 5-15 seconds, and repeat for the duration of the workout. Total distance will be about 10-16 laps.

Time: 10-15 minutes

Effort: RPE 2-3; 60-69% max HR. You should be able to talk easily with a training partner.

COOL-DOWN: Swim the final two laps very slowly. Finish with 5 minutes of stretching.

CALORIES BURNED: 120-170

COMMENTS

This workout helps to maintain balance within different muscles. It is also a great recovery workout when you are further along in your training. Vary the strokes among the crawl, breaststroke, and backstroke.

WORKOUT 5

EASY SKIING WITH SMALL HILLS
TOTAL TIME: 25-35 minutes

WARM-UP: Slowly, over about 5 minutes, let your HR rise up to 70% of max.

WORKOUT

Winter activity: Classic skiing on terrain with small, gentle hills lasting 30-60 seconds

Summer activity: Brisk walking on a trail with some small hills

Exerciser: Ski simulator set at moderately low resistance. Set level to give you an HR at 70% of max. Occasionally, for 30-60 seconds, pull slightly harder so your heart rate goes up 5-10 beats.

Distance: 2-3K, but no more

Time: 12-18 minutes

Effort: RPE 3-4; 65-74% max HR. You should be able to talk in full sentences.

COOL-DOWN: For the final 5 minutes, reduce your pace, but be sure to keep your legs moving. Finish with 5 minutes of stretching.

CALORIES BURNED: 175-225

COMMENTS

You will slow down when going up the hills. This is a relatively steady state workout, but the uphill climbs will raise your HR slightly and the downhill glides will give you a little rest.

WORKOUT 6

6

EASY SKIING WITH SMALL HILLS
TOTAL TIME: 30-40 minutes

WARM-UP: Slowly, over about 5 minutes, let your HR rise up to 70% of max.

WORKOUT

Winter activity: Classic skiing on a gently rolling trail with a few easy hills

Summer activity: Walking with long steps with poles in gently hilly area

Exerciser: Ski simulator set at moderately low resistance. Set level to give you an HR at 70% of max. During the workout, vary the intensity a little so that your heart rate occasionally climbs a little higher and occasionally falls a little lower.

Distance: 3-4K

Time: 18-24 minutes

Effort: RPE 3-4; 65-74% max HR. You should be able to talk in full sentences.

COOL-DOWN: Reduce your speed for the last 5 minutes so that your heart rate drops. Be sure to keep moving during this period. Finish with 5 minutes of stretching.

CALORIES BURNED: 245-320

COMMENTS

Try to keep your heart rate at a steady state during this workout. Slow down enough on the uphills that your heart rate does not go over 75% of max. On the downhill glides it should fall back to 65% of max HR or lower.

WORKOUT 7

EASY RUN
TOTAL TIME: 20-25 minutes

WARM-UP: Start walking. Gradually increase your speed over 5 minutes, until your HR reaches 70% of max.

WORKOUT

Winter activity: Easy running
Summer activity: Easy running
Distance: 1.5-2.5K, but no more
Time: 10-15 minutes
Effort: RPE 3-4; 65-74% max HR. You should be able to talk in full sentences.

COOL-DOWN: Five minutes of gradually decreasing intensity. Walk easily for the final couple of minutes. Finish with 5 minutes of stretching.

CALORIES BURNED: 150-200

COMMENTS

This is an easy run or jog and is meant to help keep muscle balance during the winter. If you cannot run for the entire distance, walk when necessary, but try to keep the entire distance at 1.5-2.5K.

8

EASY SKIING
TOTAL TIME: 30-35 minutes

WARM-UP: Slowly, over about 5 minutes, let your HR rise up to 75% of max.

WORKOUT

Winter activity: Classic skiing on a gently rolling ski trail

Summer activity: In-line skating or easy running

Exerciser: Ski simulator set at moderately low resistance. Set level to give you an HR at 70% of max. During the workout, vary the intensity a little so your heart rate occasionally climbs a little higher and falls a little lower.

Distance: 2-3K

Time: 15-20 minutes

Effort: RPE 3-4; 65-74% max HR. You should be able to talk in full sentences.

COOL-DOWN: Spend the final 5 minutes skiing very slowly and allowing your HR to decrease as much as possible while you're still moving. Finish with 5 minutes of stretching.

CALORIES BURNED: 245-325

COMMENTS

An RPE of 4 is slightly intense. As you ski over the hills, slow down if your heart rate is going much over 75% of your max. If you can't maintain a steady pace, slow down briefly and then bring your HR back up.

WORKOUT 9

EASY SKIING
TOTAL TIME: 35-40 minutes

WARM-UP: Slowly, over about 5 minutes, let your HR rise up to 70% of max.

WORKOUT

Winter activity: Classic skiing on a gently rolling trail

Summer activity: Bike riding on a rolling trail or road, without long or hard climbs

Distance: 3-4K

Time: 20-25 minutes

Effort: RPE 3-4; 65-74% max HR. You should be able to talk in full sentences.

COOL-DOWN: Use 5 minutes to gradually decrease your speed until your HR has decreased and you feel relaxed. Finish with 5 minutes of stretching.

CALORIES BURNED: 325-400

COMMENTS

Focus on keeping a relatively steady HR throughout the workout. Adjust your speed to fit the terrain so that your HR does not exceed 75% of your maximum for more than a few seconds at a time. Use your arms some to help maintain your glide.

WORKOUT 10

10

EASY NATURAL INTERVALS
TOTAL TIME: 40-50 minutes

WARM-UP: Slowly, over about 5 minutes, let your HR rise up to 70% of max.

WORKOUT

Winter activity: Classic skiing on gently rolling trails
Summer activity: Hiking with poles on gently rolling trails
Exerciser: Ski simulator set at moderate resistance. Set level to give you an HR of 70-74% of max. Try to increase and decrease your arm work during the workout to allow your legs to maintain a consistent effort.
Distance: 3-5K
Time: 25-30 minutes
Effort: RPE 4; 70-74% max HR. You should be able to talk in full sentences.

COOL-DOWN: Spend 5-7 minutes at the end of the workout at a very easy level to allow your body to cool down. Be sure to keep your arms and legs moving. Finish with 5 minutes of stretching.

CALORIES BURNED: 375-475

COMMENTS

Natural intervals mean that you will try to keep your speed somewhat constant, even up the hills. For this workout, choose trails with only gentle hills. Reduce your speed if your HR rises to more than 80% of max on the uphills. This workout should still be easy, with very short sections where you are not able to talk in full sentences. It is better to keep the intensity too low than too high.

7

Blue Zone

The Green zone introduced you to low-intensity training and allowed your muscles and cardiovascular system to adapt to training. The Blue zone offers the same training intensity, but the duration is increased so you'll begin to reap the benefits of low-intensity, longer duration workouts.

All Blue zone workouts are low intensity, but the duration varies from 30 minutes to long tours lasting three or more hours. I encourage you to occasionally do some of the longer, low-intensity workouts. It may take some time to build up to them, but eventually you'll be successful. Elite athletes spend as much as 80 percent of their time doing low-intensity, long duration training.

It is through the Blue zone workouts that your muscles begin to adapt to aerobic exercise. You'll develop more capillaries, which increase the blood flow to your muscles. Additionally, your aerobic enzymes will increase, and you will be able to more efficiently use oxygen in metabolizing carbohydrates and fats.

1

VERY EASY SKIING
TOTAL TIME: 45-55 minutes

WARM-UP: Slowly, over about 5 minutes, let your HR rise up to 65% of max.

WORKOUT

Winter activity: Classic skiing on level terrain

Summer activity: Brisk walking with some jogging

Exerciser: Ski simulator set at low resistance. Set level to give you an HR at 65% of max.

Distance: 4-7K

Time: 30-40 minutes

Effort: RPE 2-3; 60-69% max HR. You should be able to talk easily with a training partner.

COOL-DOWN: Slow down during the final 5 minutes until you're walking on your skis. Finish with 5 minutes of stretching.

CALORIES BURNED: 380-400

COMMENTS

Go at an intensity that you know is easy. Your speed will fluctuate depending on snow conditions and your ability. Vary your speed from a walk on skis to an easy glide. As soon as you feel your heart rate going up beyond 70%, be sure to back off and slow down again. This workout may be done on a packed trail or touring in the woods. If you can't keep your heart rate down while maintaining a glide, alternate a few minutes of skiing with a few minutes of walking on your skis.

VERY EASY SKIING
TOTAL TIME: 70-80 minutes

2

WARM-UP: Slowly, over about 5 minutes, let your HR rise up to 65% of max.

WORKOUT

Winter activity: Classic skiing on level terrain

Summer activity: Walking with poles and pushing a little on the poles

Exerciser: Ski simulator set at low resistance. Set level to give you an HR at 65% of max.

Distance: 7-10K, but no more

Time: 50-60 minutes

Effort: RPE 2-3; 60-69% max HR. You should be able to talk easily with a training partner.

COOL-DOWN: Slow down over the final 5 minutes. Finish with 10 minutes of stretching. Focus on calf muscles, hamstrings, and arms.

CALORIES BURNED: 620-740

COMMENTS

Try to maintain a steady pace. Do not graduate to longer workouts until you can maintain a steady pace for this entire distance. Your ability and the snow conditions will determine the speed and distance that you go.

WORKOUT 3

3

VERY EASY SKIING
TOTAL TIME: 95-110 minutes

WARM-UP: Slowly, over about 5 minutes, let your HR rise up to 65% of max.

WORKOUT

Winter activity: Classic skiing on level terrain

Summer activity: Bike riding on flat trails

Exerciser: Ski simulator set at low resistance. Set level to give you an HR at 65% of max.

Distance: 10-15K

Time: 75-90 minutes

Effort: RPE 2-3; 60-69% max HR. You should be able to talk easily with a training partner.

COOL-DOWN: During the last 5 minutes, reduce the speed and intensity. Finish with 10 minutes of stretching. Use the entire set of 10 stretches covered in chapter 5.

CALORIES BURNED: 920-1,100

COMMENTS

When you can finish this workout without stopping, you can be sure that your aerobic base development is progressing very well.

WORKOUT 4

SWIMMING
TOTAL TIME: 45-55 minutes

WARM-UP: Slowly, over about 5 minutes, let your HR rise up to 65% of max.

WORKOUT

Winter activity: Swimming in a 25-meter pool

Summer activity: Swimming in a 25-meter pool

Distance: Do any stroke for 100 meters 4 laps, rest 15-30 seconds, and repeat for the duration of the workout. Total distance will be about 25-40 laps.

Time: 30-40 minutes

Effort: RPE 2-3; 60-69% max HR. You would be able to talk easily, if swimming permitted it.

COOL-DOWN: Swim the final 4 laps very slowly. Finish with 10 minutes of stretching.

CALORIES BURNED: 320-420

COMMENTS

This workout helps to maintain a balance between your different muscles. Vary the strokes among the crawl, breaststroke, and backstroke. If 4 laps between rests are too much, swim whatever distance you can without stopping, and then take a short rest. You can also vary the length of the intervals between 2 laps and 6 laps.

WORKOUT 5

EASY SKIING WITH SMALL HILLS
TOTAL TIME: 50-60 minutes

WARM-UP: Slowly, over about 5 minutes, let your HR rise up to 70% of max.

WORKOUT

Winter activity: Classic skiing on terrain with small, gentle hills lasting 30-60 seconds

Summer activity: Brisk walking on a trail with some small hills

Exerciser: Ski simulator set on a moderately low resistance. Set level to give you an HR at 70% of max. Occasionally, pull slightly harder for 30-60 seconds so your heart rate goes up 5-10 beats.

Distance: 5-8K

Time: 30-40 minutes

Effort: RPE 3-4; 65-74% max HR. You should be able to talk in full sentences.

COOL-DOWN: Reduce your pace for the final 5 minutes, but be sure to keep your legs moving. Finish with 10 minutes of stretching.

CALORIES BURNED: 470-620

COMMENTS

You will slow down when going up the hills. This workout keeps your HR at a relatively steady state, but the uphill climbs will raise your HR slightly and the downhill glides will give you a little rest.

WORKOUT 6

3-HOUR DISTANCE SKI
TOTAL TIME: 205-215 minutes

6

WARM-UP: Begin the workout with 10-15 minutes of very easy skiing. If any muscles feel tight, stop and stretch at any time during the workout.

WORKOUT

Winter activity: Skating or classic skiing on a prepared track

Summer activity: Hiking on trails at a brisk pace or while carrying a 10- to 15-lb pack

Distance: As far as you can ski in 3 hours at an easy intensity

Time: 3 hours, but be willing to go shorter or longer, depending on how you feel.

Effort: RPE 3-4; 65-74% max HR. You should be able to talk in full sentences and to sing on downhills.

COOL-DOWN: Slow down over the final 10-15 minutes, although you will probably already be going slow. Finish with 5 minutes of stretching.

CALORIES BURNED: About 2,900-4,500

COMMENTS

This is a great workout to do with a group of friends. Plan this workout for a day when you want to do an off-trail tour. If you go off trail, be sure to let someone know where you are going, and don't go alone. Be sure to take food and drink along with you and eat and drink a little every 20-30 minutes.

5-HOUR DISTANCE SKI
TOTAL TIME: 5 hours or more

WARM-UP: Begin the workout with 10-15 minutes of very easy skiing. If any muscles feel tight, stop and stretch at any time during the workout.

WORKOUT

Winter activity: Skating or classic skiing on a long prepared track, or off-trail touring

Summer activity: Long bike tour

Distance: As far as you can ski in 5 hours at an easy intensity

Time: 5 hours, but be willing to go shorter or longer, depending on how you feel.

Effort: RPE 3-4; 65-74% max HR. You should be able to talk in full sentences.

COOL-DOWN: Slow down to very easy skiing for the final 5-10 minutes. Finish with 5 minutes of stretching.

CALORIES BURNED: About 4,200-6,000

COMMENTS

You will need to eat and drink during this workout. Bring a pack with fruit, energy bars, plenty of fluid, and dry clothes. When you are done, be sure to change into dry clothes right away and to eat a large mixed meal.

WORKOUT 8

EASY JOG OR RUN
TOTAL TIME: 50-55 minutes

8

WARM-UP: Slowly, over about 5 minutes, let your HR rise up to 70% of max.

WORKOUT

Winter activity: Running or jogging on a gently rolling trail
Summer activity: Running or jogging on a gently rolling trail
Distance: 5-8K
Time: 30-35 minutes
Effort: RPE 4; 70-74% max HR. You should be able to talk in nearly full sentences.

COOL-DOWN: Spend the final 5 minutes reducing your speed to a walk. Finish with 10 minutes of stretching.

CALORIES BURNED: 500-580

COMMENTS

An RPE of 4 is somewhat heavy training. As you run over the hills, slow down if your heart rate is going much over 75% of your max. If you can't maintain a steady pace, slow down for short sections and then bring your HR back up.

WORKOUT 9

9

EASY NATURAL INTERVALS
TOTAL TIME: 50-60 minutes

WARM-UP: Slowly, over about 5 minutes, let your HR rise up to 70% of max.

WORKOUT

Winter activity: Classic skiing on gently rolling trails
Summer activity: Bike riding on a rolling trail or road with no long or hard climbs
Distance: 4-7K skiing or 10-16K biking
Time: 30-40 minutes
Effort: RPE 3-4; 65-74% max HR. You should be able to talk in full sentences.

COOL-DOWN: Use 5 minutes to gradually decrease your speed until your HR has decreased and you feel relaxed. Finish with 10 minutes of stretching.

CALORIES BURNED: 500-660

COMMENTS

The focus is to keep a relatively steady speed throughout the workout. Adjust your speed on the uphills so that your HR does not exceed 75% of your max for more than a few seconds at a time. Use your arms some to help maintain your glide while skiing.

WORKOUT 10

EASY NATURAL INTERVALS
TOTAL TIME: 70-85 minutes

10

WARM-UP: Slowly, over about 5 minutes, let your HR rise up to 70% of max.

WORKOUT

Winter activity: Classic skiing on a gently rolling ski trail

Summer activity: Hiking with poles on gently rolling trails

Exerciser: Ski simulator set on a moderately low resistance. Set level to give you an HR at 75% of max. Increase and decrease your arm work during the workout so that your legs maintain a consistent effort.

Distance: 7-10K

Time: 50-60 minutes

Effort: RPE 4; 70-74% max HR. You should be able to talk in full sentences.

COOL-DOWN: Spend 5-7 minutes at the end of the workout at a very easy level to allow your body to cool down. Be sure to keep your arms and legs moving. Finish with 10 minutes of stretching.

CALORIES BURNED: 750-900

COMMENTS

With these natural intervals, you will try to keep your speed somewhat constant, even up the hills. Choose trails with only gentle hills for this workout. If your HR gets to more than 80% of max on the uphills, reduce your speed. This should still be a low-intensity workout with very short sections where you are not able to talk in full sentences. It is better to keep the intensity too low rather than too high. You may be quite tired after this workout.

8

Purple Zone

In the Purple zone, workout intensity moves into the medium range. Your heart rate will be between 75 percent and 89 percent of maximum. There are a few natural interval workouts where your heart rate may actually approach 95 percent or more of your maximum heart rate for short periods of time. The workouts are all 30 minutes or less.

The Purple zone introduces skate skiing workouts. Skate skiing—even easy skating—has a higher work threshold than classic skiing. This zone also introduces modest speed work and pace training. If you are thinking about doing any racing, you'll find that the workouts in this zone will help you reach a new level of fitness, they'll infuse variety into your workouts, and they'll make you sweat.

Most longer races require an intensity equivalent to the recommended intensity of the Purple zone workouts, while the shorter, 5K races may be in the harder zones—above 90 percent of maximum heart rate. Cross-country ski races longer than 7.5K tend to be mostly aerobic and will be at or below 90 percent of max HR.

Interval Training

Because of the many variables associated with speed in cross-country skiing, base your Purple zone intervals on percentage of max HR until you have a good feel for the RPE at different HR levels. At that time, you can begin to base the intervals on RPE.

The intervals in the Purple zone will not feel difficult. They are the equivalent speed of a 10K to 50K race, skiing about 1/10th to 1/20th of the distance, each interval just slightly faster than your current race pace and then getting a full rest. The advantages of interval training are many:

- Intervals prepare your body for a slightly faster speed without the stress of long, high-intensity workouts.
- Intervals allow you to train at a pace slightly faster than race speed without becoming overly fatigued.
- The length of the intervals can be easily varied, making your training more interesting.
- Intervals teach you to feel the proper race pace.
- You can do more high-intensity training in one workout using intervals with rest than you could do at steady state. This allows you more time skiing at a race intensity, or faster, helping you to improve more quickly.
- Interval workouts are the best workouts for improving your VO_2max.

I recommend that during the recovery time between intervals, you continue to ski at a very easy intensity for the distance of the interval. The total distance covered in Purple zone workouts is about 2K to 5K excluding warm-up, cool-down, and recovery periods.

Purple zone intervals should feel reasonably comfortable if you don't maintain them for too long; they're not maximal efforts. You should be working at a speed where normal conversation is difficult, but you should still be able to talk in short sentences when necessary. You shouldn't have to concentrate on your effort, and your mind may wander without losing skiing speed. The easiest way to summarize this intensity is that you feel like you're beginning to push yourself and breathe harder, but you recover quickly if you keep the distance short. Many endurance athletes will naturally choose a Purple zone intensity when they go out for a workout. If you have not done many intervals before, these sessions may seem quite hard at first. Focus on relaxing and skiing fast, but not hard.

Intervals need to be preceded by a good warm-up. The warm-up is generally an easy ski of about 5 minutes, and then another 5 to 10 minutes of gradually increasing speed. After you are warm, do three or four 10-second, relaxed speed bursts; then you'll be ready to do your intervals. It's important to finish an interval workout with a cool-down of 5 to 10 minutes of easy skiing.

The Purple zone uses three types of interval workouts:

- **Long intervals.** These are intervals longer than 1K. They are done just above your current pace for a 20K race, which feels quite easy. The recovery period is generally about three to four minutes long. Be careful not to do these at more than about 85 percent to 90 percent of maximum heart rate.
- **Medium intervals.** These are intervals of 250 meters to 1K, taking about 40 seconds to 5 minutes. Do these at a slightly faster than 5K race pace and at about 90 percent to 92 percent of max HR. Make the recovery period at least two minutes or the length of the interval, whichever is more.
- **Short intervals.** These intervals take 30 seconds or less. They're done faster than the medium intervals, but not quite at maximum effort. The effort needs to be relaxed, but fast. Because of the intervals' short duration, your heart rate may not be extremely high until the end of the workout. Don't worry about your heart rate for short intervals, but rather focus on a high-intensity effort for the duration of the short interval, followed by two minutes of easy skiing to fully recover. During the recovery, be sure that your heart rate falls to below 60 percent of max.

Pace Training

Pace training helps you increase the speed at which you cover a given distance. By systematically increasing your speed over intervals, you'll eventually train yourself to maintain a higher speed for the entire training distance, such as a 5K.

Two terms are used in pace training: *race pace* and *current pace.* Race pace, also called *goal pace,* is the speed you wish to reach for the coming season, and current pace, also known as *date pace,* is the pace you could race at today.

Of course, race pace and current pace depend on the length of the event you are focusing on. Technique, equipment, type of snow, temperature, and the hills in the course also affect your speed and make it very difficult to set firm speed goals in cross-country skiing.

The bottom line: To go faster than you are currently going, you must do some training at higher speeds. These training sessions are always done as intervals, so that you go for a short distance, say 1K, slightly faster than you could currently race a full 5K course. Rest to full recovery, then do another interval. Continue this interval pattern. By practicing a new speed, you learn the technique to go faster, develop neuromuscular coordination, and stimulate changes in your cardiovascular and muscular systems that allow you to handle the higher stress to your body. As your current race speed increases, so also will the interval speed.

Even though snow speed varies daily, it is still useful to have a standard loop that you test yourself on periodically. For Purple zone training, however, I'll use RPE and HR to set training intensity. Both measures of work intensity are valuable for training when applied to the standard loop. The net result of pace training is that you'll be able to gradually improve your skiing speed without increasing your perceived effort or heart rate.

You will see many of these workouts again in the Yellow zone. There the intensity is similar, but the workouts are longer—generally 30 minutes or more. You will also see more intervals in the Orange and Red zones.

WORKOUT 1

STEADY STATE SKIING
TOTAL TIME: 35-40 minutes

WARM-UP: 10 minutes very easy skiing on a flat trail, slowly increasing HR up to 75% of max

WORKOUT

Winter activity: Skating or classic technique on a gentle, groomed trail

Summer activity: Double poling at steady state on in-line skates

Exerciser: Steady state workout on a ski simulator

Distance: 2K or more, depending on your ability

Time: 15-20 minutes

Effort: RPE 5-6; 75-84% max HR. At this intensity you can think clearly.

COOL-DOWN: 5 minutes of easy skiing on the flats followed by 5 minutes of stretching

CALORIES BURNED: About 290-380

COMMENTS

If you're skiing in hills, you may have to slow down greatly on the uphills and work harder on the flats and downhills to keep your heart rate relatively constant. Try to ski continuously. If you can't maintain the intensity for the entire workout, slow down a little.

WORKOUT 2

2

STEADY STATE SKIING
TOTAL TIME: 40-45 minutes

WARM-UP: 10 minutes very easy skiing on a flat trail, slowly increasing HR up to 75% of max

---

WORKOUT

Winter activity: Skating or classic technique on a gentle, groomed trail

Summer activity: Running on gently rolling or flat trails

Exerciser: Steady state workout on a ski simulator or rowing machine

Distance: 3K or more, depending on your ability

Time: 20-25 minutes

Effort: RPE 5-6; 75-84% max HR. At this intensity you can think clearly.

COOL-DOWN: 5 minutes of easy skiing on the flats followed by 5 minutes of stretching

CALORIES BURNED: About 380-470

COMMENTS

Ski relaxed. This should be a very rewarding workout. You'll feel like you're training, but not so intensely that you're really pushing hard. You should be able to think clearly and solve the problems of the world.

WORKOUT 3

STEADY STATE SKIING
TOTAL TIME: 45-50 minutes

3

WARM-UP: 10 minutes very easy skiing on a flat trail, slowly increasing HR up to 75% of max

WORKOUT

Winter activity: Skating or classic technique on a gentle groomed trail

Summer activity: Double poling at steady state on in-line skates

Exerciser: Steady state workout on a ski simulator

Distance: 4K or more, depending on your ability

Time: 25-30 minutes

Effort: RPE 5-6; 75-84% max HR. At this intensity you can think clearly.

COOL-DOWN: 5 minutes of easy skiing on the flats, followed by 5 minutes of stretching

CALORIES BURNED: About 470-560

COMMENTS

Finish the workout feeling a little tired, but refreshed. You should recover from this workout and feel great within an hour. If you feel tired all day, you're not ready yet for a workout this difficult. Modify the workout by keeping your intensity lower or taking short rests during the workout.

WORKOUT 4

UPPER-BODY CIRCUIT STRENGTH TRAINING

TOTAL TIME: 45-55 minutes

WARM-UP: 10 minutes of easy jogging or exercise that raises your heart rate and body temperature followed by 10 minutes of stretching

WORKOUT

Activity: Circuit strength workout. Select a combination of 4-5 exercises that strengthen the upper body.

Time: 20-30 minutes

Effort: Use weights light enough that you can do 20-30 repetitions before your muscles are fatigued. Try to do 2 sets of 4-5 exercises with 1 minute rest between exercises. Do the lifts quickly.

COOL-DOWN: 5 minutes of stretching

CALORIES BURNED: About 250-300

COMMENTS

Sample exercises include bent-knee sit-ups, push-ups, pull-ups, dips, back extensions, work on a roller board, or any set of resistance exercises that use light weights or machines. If you need greater strength gains, work with a qualified instructor to set up appropriate exercises for cross-country skiing. Use more resistance so that you can do only 8-12 repetitions of an exercise. Take at least 2 minutes of rest between each exercise.

WORKOUT 5

NATURAL INTERVALS
TOTAL TIME: 40-45 minutes

WARM-UP: Stretching indoors for 5 minutes followed by 10 minutes very easy skiing on a flat trail, slowly increasing HR up to 75% of max

WORKOUT

Winter activity: Skating or classic technique on a groomed trail of rolling hills

Summer activity: In-line skating poles optional on a hilly trail

Exerciser: Ski simulator, varying the intensity to keep heart rate between 70-85% max HR

Distance: 2K or more, depending on your ability

Time: 15-20 minutes

Effort: RPE 6-7; 80-89% max HR during uphills. You need to focus and cannot talk. RPE 2-3; 60-69% max HR on flats and downhills. Recover to talking in full sentences.

COOL-DOWN: 5 minutes of easy skiing on the flats followed by 5 minutes of stretching indoors

CALORIES BURNED: About 300-400

COMMENTS

Natural intervals use the terrain to dictate your intensity. Try to recover on the downhills and ski very relaxed on the flat areas. Ski at a pace you can maintain up the hills, but one that will raise your heart rate very high by the end of the uphill. If you don't have a course with many hills, do a workout where you push hard when you feel like it, and then recover as you need to. This is called a fartlek, or *speed play,* workout.

WORKOUT 6

6

NATURAL INTERVALS
TOTAL TIME: 45-50 minutes

WARM-UP: Stretching indoors for 5 minutes followed by 10 minutes of very easy skiing on a flat trail, slowly increasing HR up to 75% of max

WORKOUT

Winter activity: Skating or classic technique on a groomed trail of rolling hills

Summer activity: Swimming. Alternate hard laps with easy laps.

Exerciser: Rowing machine or ski simulator, varying intensity to keep heart rate between 70-85% max HR

Distance: 3K or more, depending on your ability

Time: 20-25 minutes

Effort: RPE 6-7; 80-89% max HR during uphills. You need to focus and cannot talk. RPE 2-3; 60-69% max HR on flats and downhills. Recover to talking in full sentences.

COOL-DOWN: 5 minutes of easy skiing on the flats followed by 5 minutes of stretching indoors

CALORIES BURNED: About 400-500

COMMENTS

If you find that you're not recovering on the downhills and flats, slow down the entire workout including the uphills just a bit so that you find an intensity that allows recovery. If it takes longer than 3 minutes to ski up a hill, slow down and relax to the top.

WORKOUT 7

NATURAL INTERVALS
TOTAL TIME: 50-55 minutes

WARM-UP: Stretching indoors for 5 minutes followed by 10 minutes very easy skiing on a flat trail, slowly increasing HR up to 75% of max

WORKOUT

Winter activity: Skating or classic technique on a groomed trail of rolling hills

Summer activity: Running with poles on a hilly trail

Exerciser: Stair climber, varying the intensity to keep heart rate between 70-85% max HR

Distance: 4K or more, depending on your ability

Time: 25-30 minutes

Effort: RPE 5-6; 75-84% max HR during uphills. You need to focus and cannot talk. RPE 2-3; 60-69% max HR on flats and downhills. Recover to talking in full sentences.

COOL-DOWN: 5 minutes of easy skiing on the flats then 5 minutes of stretching indoors

CALORIES BURNED: About 470-560

COMMENTS

This is a good workout for moderately fit cross-country skiers who want to improve their hill climbing. The calories burned depend on your technique and skiing efficiency, but in general, this level of intensity will burn about 16-20 calories per minute. More proficient skiers will simply go farther and faster in the 25 minutes. If it takes longer than 3 minutes to ski any hill, slow down and relax to the top. Coast and recover on the downhills.

WORKOUT 8

8

SHORT INTERVALS
TOTAL TIME: 40-55 minutes

WARM-UP: Stretching indoors for 5 minutes followed by 10 minutes very easy skiing on a flat trail, slowly increasing HR up to 80% of max

WORKOUT

Winter activity: Skating or classic technique on a groomed trail of rolling hills with a 1K section you can repeat

Summer activity: Running or hill bounding with poles

Exerciser: Stair climber at a high work load for short bursts

Distance: About 4-8K of skiing, including intervals and recovery

Time: 15-30 minutes. Alternate 10- to 30-second intervals with 2-3 minutes of recovery between intervals, depending on how you feel. Stop when you are tired.

Effort: RPE 8-9; 90-99% max HR during interval. You need to focus and cannot talk. RPE 2-3; 60-69% max HR during recovery. Recover to talking in full sentences.

COOL-DOWN: 5 minutes of easy skiing on the flats then 5 minutes of stretching indoors

CALORIES BURNED: About 200-250

COMMENTS

This workout develops speed and power as you work at nearly maximal effort. Perform these intervals well above race speed, but with good technique—flowing and relaxed. To stay relaxed, focus on keeping your face and neck loose during the intervals. You'll do only 4-10 maximum-effort intervals, so the total distance at high speed will actually be very low. Don't worry about your heart rate during these high-speed intervals. Because the intervals are so short, your heart rate during the interval may not reach the target zone. Stop the intervals and cool down when you're tired and can no longer do the intervals with good technique.

WORKOUT 9

MEDIUM INTERVALS
TOTAL TIME: 40-55 minutes

9

WARM-UP: Stretching indoors for 5 minutes followed by 10 minutes of very easy skiing on a flat trail, slowly increasing HR up to 80% of max

WORKOUT

Winter activity: Skating or classic technique on any groomed trail with a 2K section you can repeat

Summer activity: Uphill hill hiking with poles to imitate the skiing workout

Exerciser: Ski simulator set to imitate the skiing workout

Distance: About 4-8K of skiing, including intervals and recovery

Time: 15-30 minutes, alternating 1- to 2-minute intervals with 2-3 minutes of recovery, depending on how you are feeling. Stop when you're tired.

Effort: RPE 7; 85-89% max HR during interval. You need to focus and cannot talk. RPE 2-3; 60-69% max HR during recovery. Recover to talking in full sentences.

COOL-DOWN: 5 minutes of easy skiing on the flats then 5 minutes of stretching indoors

CALORIES BURNED: About 300-350

COMMENTS

Do the intervals in this workout at about 5K race speed, but with good rests after short sections. Keep moving slowly between intervals to get your heart rate to recover to about 60% of max. The intervals will feel moderately hard, but don't exceed the target HR. Focus on your task at hand and stay flowing and relaxed. You should try to do 3-7 of these intervals during this workout.

WORKOUT 10

10

LONG INTERVALS
TOTAL TIME: 40-55 minutes

WARM-UP: Stretching indoors for 5 minutes followed by 10 minutes of very easy skiing on a flat trail, slowly increasing HR up to 80% of max

WORKOUT

Winter activity: Skating or classic technique on any groomed trail with a 2-3K section that you can repeat

Summer activity: Biking in hills to simulate the ski workout

Exerciser: Ski simulator set to imitate the ski workout

Distance: About 4-8K of skiing, including intervals and recovery

Time: 15-30 minutes, alternating 3- to 5-minute intervals with 2-3 minutes of recovery skiing, depending on how you feel. Stop when you are tired.

Effort: RPE 6; 80-84% max HR during interval. You need to focus and cannot talk. RPE 2-3; 60-69% max HR during recovery. Recover to talking in full sentences.

COOL-DOWN: 5 minutes of easy skiing on the flats then 5 minutes of stretching indoors.

CALORIES BURNED: About 325-400

COMMENTS

This workout develops a feel for race speed. Do the intervals at about 20K race speed, not extremely hard, for about 1K at a time. Try to do them with good effort, but stay flowing and relaxed. Do the intervals on different sections of the trail for variety. Stay light and quick on your feet. You'll do only 2-4 intervals during this workout, so the distance at race pace will be only 2-4K.

9

Yellow Zone

The Yellow zone is best for athletes who are training for races from 7.5K to marathon distances. The content and intensity of the Yellow workouts are similar to those in the Purple zone, but they're longer and include many more intervals.

You should feel comfortable doing the intervals in the Purple zone before you attempt the interval workouts in this zone. If you struggled with the Purple zone workouts but you want to compete in races longer than 5-10K you can still try the workouts in the Yellow zone. Reduce the recommended heart rate range by 5 to15 beats per minute and the recommended RPE value by one point so you can finish 30 to 35 minutes of the intervals and recoveries. The planned intensity of the Yellow workouts varies with the interval length. I suggest RPE values of 8 to 9 for short intervals, 7 for medium intervals, and 6 for long intervals.

The intervals in the Yellow zone improve your power, endurance, and cardiovascular system. Always listen to your body. When you can no longer maintain your time or speed for the interval without really putting yourself under, it's time to stop for the day.

WORKOUT 1

STEADY STATE SKIING
TOTAL TIME: 55-65 minutes

WARM-UP: 10 minutes of very easy skiing on a flat trail, slowly increasing HR up to 75% of max

WORKOUT

Winter activity: Skating or classic skiing on a gentle prepared trail

Summer activity: Double poling at a steady state on in-line skates. Go easy and work those arms.

Exerciser: Steady state workout on a ski exerciser

Distance: 5K or more, depending on your ability

Time: 30-40 minutes

Effort: RPE 5-6; 75-84% max HR. At this intensity you can think clearly.

COOL-DOWN: 10 minutes of easy skiing on the flats followed by 5 minutes of stretching

CALORIES BURNED: About 560-740

COMMENTS

Try to maintain the same intensity throughout the workout. If skiing in hills, you may have to slow down greatly on the uphills and work harder on the flats and downhills to keep your heart rate relatively constant. If you can't maintain the intensity for the entire workout, slow down a little.

WORKOUT 2

STEADY STATE SKIING

TOTAL TIME: 65-75 minutes

WARM-UP: 10 minutes of easy skiing on a flat trail, slowly increasing HR up to 75% of max

WORKOUT

Winter activity: Skating or classic skiing on a gentle prepared trail

Summer activity: Running on gentle rolling or flat trails

Exerciser: Steady state workout on a ski simulator or rowing machine

Distance: 6K or more, depending on your ability

Time: 40-50 minutes

Effort: RPE 5-6; 75-84% max HR. At this intensity you can think clearly.

COOL-DOWN: 10 minutes of easy skiing on the flats followed by 5 minutes of stretching

CALORIES BURNED: About 740-900

COMMENTS

Remember to do this workout at below race intensity. You should feel relaxed, but like you are getting a moderate workout. It is important not to go too hard and to maintain the pace.

3

STEADY STATE SKIING

TOTAL TIME: 80-90 minutes

WARM-UP: 10 minutes of easy skiing on a flat trail, slowly increasing HR up to 75% of max

WORKOUT

Winter activity: Skating or classic skiing on a gentle prepared trail
Summer activity: Biking at a steady state on flat or gently rolling roads. Keep it spinning.
Exerciser: Steady state workout on a ski simulator
Distance: 8K or more, depending on your ability
Time: 50-60 minutes
Effort: RPE 5-6; 75-84% max HR. At this intensity you can think clearly.

COOL-DOWN: 10 minutes of easy skiing on the flats followed by 10 minutes of stretching

CALORIES BURNED: About 920-1,100

COMMENTS

You'll feel quite tired at the end of this workout, but you'll recover within an hour or two and feel great. If you feel tired all day, you're not yet ready for a workout this difficult and you need to keep your intensity lower or take short rests during the workout.

WORKOUT 4

PLYOMETRIC AND LEG POWER TRAINING

TOTAL TIME: 60 minutes

WARM-UP: 10 minutes of easy jogging or exercise that raises your heart rate and body temperature followed by 10 minutes of stretching focused on your legs

WORKOUT

Activity: Plyometric strength workout. Select a combination of 4-5 plyometric exercises that focus on developing leg strength.

Time: 30 minutes total time, alternating 30 seconds of an activity with 2 minutes of rest before the next exercise. Try to do 2 sets of 4-5 exercises.

Effort: Try to do the exercises explosively. For example, jump as many stairs as you can safely, select a barrier that's a challenging height, and achieve good distance on the side jumps. The muscles you use should be fatigued within 30 seconds.

COOL-DOWN: 10 minutes of stretching

CALORIES BURNED: About 250-300

COMMENTS

Plyometrics include a great variety of jumps, some requiring good leg strength. Here are some suggestions: Jump up 1-4 stairs at a time with both legs; jump from side to side over a 5- to 15-inch barrier; do repeated vertical jumps in place; run in place, lifting your knees as high as possible; run in place, lifting your heels to kick your buttocks; hop as far as you can from side to side. If you wish to use more advanced plyometrics, such as depth jumps or jumps that require more eccentric muscle activity, for greater power gains, get a good manual on plyometrics or work with an instructor to set up appropriate plyometric and leg power exercises for cross-country skiing.

5 NATURAL INTERVALS

TOTAL TIME: 60-70 minutes

WARM-UP: Stretching indoors for 5 minutes followed by 10 minutes of easy skiing on a flat trail, slowly increasing HR up to 75% of max

WORKOUT

Winter activity: Skating or classic skiing on a prepared trail with rolling hills

Summer activity: In-line skating, poles optional, on a hilly trail

Exerciser: Ski simulator, varying the intensity to keep your heart rate between 70-85% of max HR

Distance: 4K or more, depending on your ability

Time: 30-40 minutes

Effort: RPE 6-7; 80-89% max HR during uphills. You need to focus and cannot talk. RPE 2-3; 60-69% max HR on flats and downhills. Recover to talking in full sentences.

COOL-DOWN: 5 minutes of easy skiing on the flats followed by 10 minutes of stretching indoors

CALORIES BURNED: About 560-740

COMMENTS

Use the terrain to dictate your intervals. Try to recover on the downhills and ski relaxed on the flat areas. Ski at a pace that you can maintain up the hill, but one that will raise your heart rate very high by the end of the uphill. If it takes longer than 3 minutes to ski up any hill, slow down and relax to the top. Coast and recover on the downhills. If you don't have a course with many hills, then do a fartlek interval workout where you push hard when you feel like it and recover as you need to.

WORKOUT 6

NATURAL INTERVALS

TOTAL TIME: 70-80 minutes

WARM-UP: Stretching indoors 5 minutes followed by 10 minutes of easy skiing on a flat trail, slowly increasing HR up to 75% of max

WORKOUT

Winter activity: Skating or classic skiing on a prepared trail with rolling hills

Summer activity: Swimming, alternating hard laps with easy laps

Exerciser: Rowing machine or ski simulator, varying intensity to keep heart rate between 70-85% max HR

Distance: 6K or more, depending on your ability

Time: 40-50 minutes

Effort: RPE 6-7; 80-89% max HR during uphills. You need to focus and cannot talk. RPE 2-3; 60-69% max HR on flats and downhills. Recover to talking in full sentences.

COOL-DOWN: 5 minutes of easy skiing on the flats followed by 10 minutes of stretching indoors

CALORIES BURNED: About 720-920

COMMENTS

If you find that you are not recovering on the downhills and flats, slow down the entire workout including the uphills just a bit so you find an intensity that allows recovery. If it takes longer than 3 minutes to ski up any hill, slow down and relax to the top.

7

NATURAL INTERVALS

TOTAL TIME: 80-90 minutes

WARM-UP: Stretching indoors for 5 minutes followed by 10 minutes of easy skiing on a flat trail, slowly increasing HR up to 75% of max

WORKOUT

Winter activity: Skating or classic skiing on a prepared trail with rolling hills

Summer activity: Running with poles on a hilly trail

Exerciser: Stair climber, varying the intensity to keep heart rate between 70-85% max HR

Distance: 8K or more, depending on your ability

Time: 50-60 minutes

Effort: RPE 5-6; 75-84% max HR during uphills. You need to focus and cannot talk. RPE 2-3; 60-69% max HR on flats and downhills. Recover to talking in full sentences.

COOL-DOWN: 5 minutes of easy skiing on the flats followed by 10 minutes of stretching indoors

CALORIES BURNED: About 920-1,100

COMMENTS

This is a good workout for fit cross-country skiers who want to improve their hill climbing and learn to make a "break-away move" on the hills. More proficient skiers will simply go farther and faster in the 50-60 minutes.

WORKOUT 8

TOTAL TIME: 65-95 minutes

WARM-UP: Stretching indoors for 5 minutes followed by 15 minutes of easy skiing on a flat trail, slowly increasing HR up to 80% of max

WORKOUT

Winter activity: Skating or classic skiing on a prepared trail with a 1K section you can repeat

Summer activity: Hill bounding with poles

Exerciser: Short bursts on a stair climber set at a high work load

Distance: About 6-15K of skiing, including intervals and recovery

Time: 30-60 minutes alternating 10- to 30-second intervals with 2-3 minutes of recovery skiing, depending on how you feel. Stop when you are tired.

Effort: RPE 8-9; 90-99% max HR during interval. You need to focus and cannot talk. RPE 2-3; 60-69% max HR during recovery. Recover to talking in full sentences.

COOL-DOWN: 10 minutes of easy skiing on the flats followed by 5 minutes of stretching indoors

CALORIES BURNED: About 350-700

COMMENTS

This workout develops speed and power. The intervals require just less than maximal effort, which may give you a very hard workout. However, if it becomes too difficult to maintain your speed, use a longer recovery period between the speed bursts. Do the intervals well above race speed with good effort and with flowing, relaxed technique. Keep your shoulders and neck loose during the intervals. The 10-25 intervals in this workout are a lot of speed work, so be sure to recover between each burst. Stop and cool down when you're tired and can't do the intervals with good technique.

MEDIUM INTERVALS

TOTAL TIME: 65-95 minutes

WARM-UP: Stretching indoors 5 minutes followed by 15 minutes of easy skiing on a flat trail, slowly increasing HR up to 80% of max

WORKOUT

Winter activity: Skating or classic skiing on a prepared trail with a 2K section you can repeat

Summer activity: Uphill hiking with poles to imitate the ski workout

Exerciser: Ski simulator workout to imitate the ski workout

Distance: About 6-15K of skiing, including intervals and recovery

Time: 30-60 minutes, alternating 1- to 2-minute intervals with 2-3 minutes of recovery, depending on how you are feeling. Stop when you're tired.

Effort: RPE 7; 84-89% max HR during interval. You need to focus and cannot talk. RPE 2-3; 60-69% max HR during recovery. Recover to talking in full sentences.

COOL-DOWN: 5 minutes of easy skiing on the flats followed by 10 minutes of stretching indoors

CALORIES BURNED: About 500-750

COMMENTS

The intervals in this workout are at about 5K race speed, but with good rests after short sections. They'll feel moderately hard at first, but be sure not to exceed the target HR. The later intervals will begin to feel harder. Try to stay relaxed. Try to do 6-15 intervals for this workout. It is a difficult workout, so reduce your intensity and increase the recovery period if necessary.

WORKOUT 10

LONG INTERVALS

TOTAL TIME: 65-95 minutes

WARM-UP: Stretching indoors for 5 minutes followed by 10 minutes of easy skiing on a flat trail, slowly increasing HR up to 80% of max

WORKOUT

Winter activity: Skating or classic skiing on a prepared trail with a 2-3K section you can repeat

Summer activity: Biking in hills to simulate the ski workout

Exerciser: Ski simulator to imitate the ski workout

Distance: About 6-15K of skiing, including intervals and recovery

Time: 30-60 minutes, alternating 3- to 5-minute intervals with 2-3 minutes of recovery skiing, depending on how you feel

Effort: RPE 6; 80-84% max HR during interval. You need to focus and cannot talk. RPE 2-3; 60-69% max HR during recovery. Recover to talking in full sentences.

COOL-DOWN: 10 minutes of easy skiing on the flats followed by 10 minutes of stretching indoors

CALORIES BURNED: About 550-800

COMMENTS

This workout develops power endurance and a feel for race speed. The intervals are at about 15-30K race speed, but for only about 1-1.5K at a time. Do them with good effort, focusing on good technique. Stay light and quick on your feet. You'll do 3-8 intervals during this workout.

10

Orange Zone

The Orange zone workouts prescribe intervals that are at or above race intensity, with RPEs of 7 to 10, but they last less than 30 minutes.

You should feel comfortable with the intervals in the Purple and Yellow zones before you try the higher-intensity intervals in this zone. It doesn't take long for the workouts in this zone to cause fatigue. Orange and Red zone workouts combine for less than 20 percent of the total training time for high-level athletes. Beginning and intermediate skiers don't need to train in these zones; the workouts are designed to improve speed and endurance for racing. The Purple and Yellow zones contain all the intervals you will ever need for aerobic fitness.

The workouts in this zone are geared to skiers who are focusing on races of 10K or shorter. Work up to doing the maximum number of intervals per workout that I recommend in the "Comments" of each workout before you move on to workouts in the Red zone.

Hard intervals need to be done when you are rested, so plan these workouts to follow easy training days. The plans in chapter 13 are arranged according to this guideline. Start the first intervals slightly slower than you believe you will be able to maintain. Try to pick up the pace on subsequent intervals or maintain the pace of the first interval. Pay attention to how you feel when you're doing hard intervals. When you can no longer maintain good technique, or if your speed is decreasing from the previous interval, it is time to rest more or to cool down and stop.

WORKOUT 1

MIXED INTERVALS
TOTAL TIME: 40-55 minutes

WARM-UP: 10 minutes of easy skiing on a flat trail, slowly increasing HR up to 75% of max. Finish your warm-up with 4 x 30 seconds of skiing with relaxed not maximal speed.

WORKOUT

Winter activity: Skating or classic skiing on a gently rolling trail with few hills

Summer activity: Running intervals as described in the skiing workout. Use a track for consistency.

Exerciser: Ski simulator imitating the skiing workout

Distance: 4.5-9K total skiing with interval and recovery skiing

Time: 13-26 minutes, divided as follows:

1 minute fast skiing, 2 minutes recovery

2 minutes fast skiing, 2 minutes recovery

3 minutes fast skiing, 3 minutes recovery

Repeat once, if able.

Effort: RPE 8-9; 90-99% max HR during interval. Need to focus on the task at hand. RPE 3-4; 65-74% max HR during recovery. Recover to talking in full sentences.

COOL-DOWN: 10 minutes of easy skiing on the flats followed by 5 minutes of stretching

CALORIES BURNED: About 400-550

COMMENTS

The 1-minute intervals should be done at about 94% of max heart rate, and the longer, 2- and 3-minute intervals can be done at about 90% of max heart rate. Focus on good skiing technique, staying relaxed and fluid. Stop when you can no longer maintain the pace.

WORKOUT 2

2

SHORT INTERVALS
TOTAL TIME: 45-60 minutes

WARM-UP: 10 minutes of easy skiing on a flat trail, slowly increasing HR up to 75% of max. Finish your warm-up with 4 x 30 seconds of skiing with relaxed not maximal speed.

WORKOUT

Winter activity: Skating or classic skiing on a gently rolling trail
Summer activity: Hill bounding with poles
Distance: 5-7K total, including interval and recovery skiing
Time: 20-30 minutes, alternating10- to 15-second bursts of all-out intensity with 1 to 1-1/2 minutes of rest. Stop earlier if very tired.
Effort: RPE 10; 100% max HR during interval. You are working at maximum effort. RPE 3-4; 65-74% max HR during recovery. Recover to talking in full sentences.

COOL-DOWN: 10 minutes of easy skiing on the flats followed by 5 minutes of stretching

CALORIES BURNED: About 350-450

COMMENTS

These all-out intervals work on power and speed. Don't worry about heart rate during these intervals, as you may not reach max HR due to the short 10-15 seconds of the interval. Focus on going as fast as you can and working as hard as you can. Relax and maintain good technique, though, because it's possible to work at a high intensity without going fast if you don't. Remember, speed is the name of the racing game. Take a longer recovery in the off-season; take a shorter recover in the race season. You may find that the first time you do these workouts you'll feel like doing only 3-4 intervals. Eventually you should be able to work up to 10-15.

WORKOUT 3

MEDIUM INTERVALS
TOTAL TIME: 45-55 minutes

3

WARM-UP: 10 minutes of easy skiing on a flat trail, slowly increasing HR up to 75% of max. Finish your warm-up with a few minutes at race pace.

WORKOUT

Winter activity: Skating or classic skiing on a gently rolling trail
Summer activity: In-line skating with poles
Exerciser: Ski simulator set to imitate the skiing workout
Distance: 6-9K total, including interval and recovery skiing
Time: 20-30 minutes, alternating 1- to 2-minute intervals just above 5K race speed with 1-2 minutes rest. Stop earlier if you're very tired.
Effort: RPE 8-9; 90-99% max HR during interval. Need to focus on the task at hand. RPE 3-4; 65-74% max HR during recovery. Recover to talking in full sentences.

COOL-DOWN: 10 minutes of easy skiing on the flats followed by 5 minutes of stretching

CALORIES BURNED: About 400-500

COMMENTS

Focus on going as fast as you can without exceeding 95% HR during the first few intervals. During later intervals, try to focus on maintaining your speed and form. Your HR may get as high as 98-99% of max. These intervals begin to help you develop a tolerance to lactic acid during a prerace peaking program. A good workout will include 5-10 intervals.

WORKOUT 4

LONG INTERVALS

TOTAL TIME: 45-55 minutes

WARM-UP: 10 minutes of easy skiing on a flat trail, slowly increasing HR up to 75% of max. Finish your warm-up with a few minutes at race pace.

WORKOUT

Winter activity: Skating or classic skiing on a gently rolling trail
Summer activity: Bike riding to simulate the skiing workout
Exerciser: Ski simulator set to imitate the skiing workout
Distance: 6-9K total, including interval and recovery skiing
Time: 20-30 minutes, alternating 3-4 minutes of skiing faster than a 5K race speed with 3-4 minutes of rest. Stop earlier if very tired.
Effort: RPE 7-8; 85-94% max HR during interval. Need to focus on the task at hand. RPE 3-4; 65-74% max HR during recovery. Recover to talking in full sentences.

COOL-DOWN: 10 minutes of easy skiing on the flats followed by 5 minutes of stretching

CALORIES BURNED: About 400-500

COMMENTS

Do these high-HR intervals on the same section of the trail each time. Start slower than planned, and then try to increase the speed on subsequent intervals until you find the highest pace you can maintain. You will find your HR getting up to 94% of max on the later intervals. Start with 1-2 intervals the first time you do this workout, and work up to 4-5.

WORKOUT 5

SHORT UPHILL INTERVALS
TOTAL TIME: 45-60 minutes

WARM-UP: 10 minutes of easy skiing on a flat trail, slowly increasing HR up to 80% of max. Finish your warm-up with 4 x 30 seconds of skiing with relaxed not maximal speed.

WORKOUT

Winter activity: Skating or classic skiing on an uphill section of trail

Summer activity: Hill bounding with poles

Distance: 5-8K total, including interval and recovery skiing

Time: 20-30 minutes, alternating 10- to 15-second bursts of all-out intensity with 1 to1-1/2 minutes of rest. Stop earlier if very tired.

Effort: RPE 10; 100% max HR during interval. You will be working as hard as possible. RPE 3-4; 65-74% max HR during recovery. Recover to talking in full sentences.

COOL-DOWN: 10 minutes of easy skiing on the flats followed by 5 minutes of stretching

CALORIES BURNED: About 350-450

COMMENTS

These are all-out intervals. Do some workouts with classic technique and use skating in other workouts. If the hill is short, gather speed on the flats and then accelerate over the top. Quality is better than quantity in these, so do as many as you can with good speed. Stop when you can no longer maintain your effort.

WORKOUT 6

MEDIUM UPHILL INTERVALS

TOTAL TIME: 45-55 minutes

WARM-UP: 10 minutes of easy skiing on a flat trail, slowly increasing HR up to 75% of max. Finish your warm-up with a few minutes at race pace.

WORKOUT

Winter activity: Skating or classic skiing on a section of trail with a hill about 0.5K long

Summer activity: In-line skating with poles to simulate the skiing workout

Exerciser: Ski simulator set to imitate the skiing workout

Distance: 5-8K total, including interval and recovery skiing

Time: 20-30 minutes, alternating 1- to 2-minute intervals at slightly faster than 5K race speed with 2-3 minutes rest. Stop earlier if very tired.

Effort: RPE 8-9; 90-99% max HR during interval. You will be working very hard, just below max. RPE 3-4; 65-74% max HR during recovery. Recover to talking in full sentences.

COOL-DOWN: 10 minutes of easy skiing on the flats followed by 5 minutes of stretching

CALORIES BURNED: About 400-500

COMMENTS

Your heart rate target is about 95% of max HR, but you might exceed this by the end of each interval. Adjust your effort based more on your perception of RPE. Focus on going as fast as you can within the target zone while still maintaining good form for the interval. Try to ski the uphills and any flats or downhills at a high speed, and maintain your speed for several intervals. Work up to being able to do 5-9 of these intervals.

WORKOUT 7

LONG UPHILL AND MIXED TERRAIN INTERVALS

TOTAL TIME: 45-55 minutes

WARM-UP: 10 minutes of easy skiing on a flat trail, slowly increasing HR up to 75% of max. Finish your warm-up with a few minutes at race pace.

WORKOUT

Winter activity: Skating or classic skiing on a section of trail with long uphills

Summer activity: Uphill hiking with poles

Exerciser: Ski simulator set to imitate the skiing workout

Distance: 5-8K total, including interval and recovery skiing

Time: 20-30 minutes, alternating 3- to 4-minute intervals at or slightly above 5K race speed with 3-4 minutes rest. Repeat until tired.

Effort: RPE 7-8; 85-94% max HR during interval. You can focus, but will be working hard. RPE 3-4; 65-74% max HR during recovery. Recover to talking in full sentences.

COOL-DOWN: 10 minutes of easy skiing on the flats followed by 5 minutes of stretching

CALORIES BURNED: About 400-500

COMMENTS

These high-max HR intervals are quite hard. Do them on the same section of trail each time. Keep your speed on the uphills and try to accelerate when the terrain changes. Treat these intervals as races, with the mind-set that you are going to do 3-4 at the same pace. Your HR may go slightly higher than 90% on the later intervals or at the end of each interval. Don't let your HR exceed 94%, but try to maintain your speed. Gradually increase the number of intervals that you do, starting with 2 and increasing to 4-5.

WORKOUT 8

8

ARMS-ONLY INTERVALS
TOTAL TIME: 45-55 minutes

WARM-UP: 10 minutes very easy skiing on a flat trail, slowly increasing HR up to 80% of max

WORKOUT

Winter activity: Double poling using arms only on a prepared trail with gentle terrain.

Summer activity: Double poling on in-line skates to imitate the skiing workout

Exerciser: On a rowing machine do a workout that imitates the skiing workout.

Distance: 4-6K total, including interval and recovery skiing

Time: 20-30 minutes, alternating 2-3 minutes of double poling on easy terrain with 3-5 minutes of recovery, using both arms and legs. Repeat until tired.

Effort: RPE 7-8; 85-94% max HR during interval. You can focus, but will be working hard. RPE 3-4; 65-74% max HR during recovery. Recover to talking in full sentences.

COOL-DOWN: 5 minutes of easy skiing on the flats followed by 10 minutes of stretching, focusing on your arms.

CALORIES BURNED: About 250-325

COMMENTS

This workout develops arm power and endurance. If you need additional resistance, do this workout up a gradual hill. If you find the double poling difficult, you might need to do strength work for your abdominals, lats, and triceps. Double-pole intervals will be at about 90% of max HR. This means that you start an interval and accelerate up to nearly full speed, maintain it for 2-3 minutes, and then relax. Keep moving during the recovery, using your arms and legs very slowly, and recover to about 65% of max HR.

WORKOUT 9

LEGS-ONLY SKATING INTERVALS

TOTAL TIME: 45-55 minutes

WARM-UP: Stretching indoors for 5 minutes, focusing on legs. Follow with 10 minutes of very easy ski skating on a flat trail, slowly increasing HR up to 80% of max.

WORKOUT

Winter activity: Skating with only legs on a hilly course

Summer activity: In-line skating uphill to imitate the skiing workout

Exerciser: Ski simulator set to imitate the skiing workout

Distance: 4-6K total, including interval and recovery skiing

Time: 20-30 minutes, alternating 2-3 minutes of skating with only legs in hilly terrain with 3-5 minutes of recovery, using both arms and legs. Repeat until tired.

Effort: RPE 7-8; 85-94% max HR during interval. You can focus, but will be working hard. RPE 3-4; 65-74% max HR during recovery. Recover to talking in full sentences.

COOL-DOWN: 5 minutes of easy skiing on the flats followed by 5 minutes of stretching indoors, focusing on your legs

CALORIES BURNED: About 400-575

COMMENTS

Intervals will be at about 90% of max effort. This means that you start an interval and accelerate up to 90% of max HR, hold for 2-3 minutes, and then relax. Keep moving between intervals, using arms and legs very slowly, and get your heart rate to recover to about 65% of max. Focus during the interval to maintain the pace. While skating, use complete leg extensions and push as far out to the side as you can. On the uphills, focus on keeping a high tempo rather than on long, hard pushes. Skate over the tops of the hills and as much as you can on easy downhills.

10

SHORT RACE
TOTAL TIME: 55-65 minutes

WARM-UP: Stretching indoors for 5 minutes followed by 10-15 minutes of very easy skiing on a flat trail, slowly increasing HR up to 80% of max. Finish with 2 to 3 15-second bursts of relaxed speed on a flat or gradual downhill.

WORKOUT

Winter activity: Classic technique or skating at 5-7.5K race pace

Summer activity: 15-25 minute race in any aerobic sport

Exerciser: 20-minute ski simulator workout at the highest intensity you can maintain

Distance: 5-7.5K

Time: 15-35 minutes, depending on ability

Effort: RPE 7-8; 85-94% max HR. You can focus, but will be working hard.

COOL-DOWN: 10 minutes of easy skiing on the flats followed by 10 minutes of stretching indoors

CALORIES BURNED: About 350-425

COMMENTS

Start at an easier pace than you think you can maintain and then increase your speed. Focus on skiing efficiently and keeping your effort up. Racing is where you learn to put it all together. Good luck.

11

Red Zone

Like the Orange zone, the Red zone covers intervals that are at race intensity and above, but the workouts last more than 30 minutes. The workouts in this zone are geared to skiers who are training for 10K or longer races.

You should feel comfortable with the shorter intervals in the Orange zone before trying the intervals in this zone. As I said earlier, most athletes, even highly trained ones, don't spend a lot of training time at this intensity, especially during the off-season periods. During the race season, you'll spend more time with these workouts because you'll be both training and racing. If you work out at this intensity, be sure also to schedule lots of rest and some easy, recovery workouts.

Do hard intervals only when you're rested; plan them following easy training days. I remind you to start the first intervals slightly slower than you believe you will be able to maintain, and then try to pick up the pace on subsequent intervals if you feel strong. Stop when you're tired and can no longer maintain the pace.

WORKOUT 1

1

DEPLETION WORKOUT WITH 5K RACE PACE

TOTAL TIME: 70-120 minutes

WARM-UP: 10 minutes of easy skiing on a flat trail, slowly increasing HR up to 75% of max. Finish your warm-up with 4 x 30 seconds of skiing at a relaxed not maximal speed.

WORKOUT

Winter activity: Skating or classic skiing on a gentle rolling trail

Summer activity: Bike riding to imitate the skiing workout

Exerciser: Ski simulator set to imitate the skiing workout, but cut distance portion in half

Distance: 10-25K total, with race pace and distance skiing

Time: 15-30 minutes of race pace skiing (5K is a good distance) followed by 30-60 minutes of very easy skiing

Effort: RPE 7-8; 85-94% max HR during 5K race pace interval. You need to focus on the task at hand. RPE 3-4; 65-74% max HR during the distance portion. You can talk in full sentences.

COOL-DOWN: 10 minutes of easy skiing on flat terrain. Finish with 5 minutes of stretching.

CALORIES BURNED: About 1,200-1,800

COMMENTS

The race pace workout will utilize much of the carbohydrates stored in your muscles. After the race pace portion, be sure to replace your carbohydrates with a sports drink or by eating some rolls and fruit. The final portion of the workout will burn fats and some carbohydrates.

WORKOUT 2

7.5K PACE TRIAL
TOTAL TIME: 55-85 minutes

2

WARM-UP: 15 minutes of easy skiing on a flat trail, slowly increasing HR up to 75% of max. Finish your warm-up with 4 x 30 seconds of skiing at a relaxed not maximal speed.

WORKOUT

Winter activity: Skating or classic skiing on any trail
Summer activity: Running in hills with poles
Distance: 7.5K at race pace
Time: 20-45 minutes
Effort: RPE 7-8; 85-94% max HR. You need to focus on the task at hand during the pace training.

COOL-DOWN: 10 minutes of easy skiing on the flats. Finish with 10 minutes of stretching.

CALORIES BURNED: About 500-800

COMMENTS

During this workout, which imitates a race, focus on maintaining an intensity you can sustain for the entire duration of the trial. Focus on how fast you can go with good technique. You will raise your heart rate a little on the hills and recover on the downhills. Use these simulated races to learn what you can do. Be willing to experiment with technique, heart rates, and pacing.

WORKOUT 3

3

10K PACE TRIAL
TOTAL TIME: 65-100 minutes

WARM-UP: 15 minutes of easy skiing on a flat trail, slowly increasing HR up to 75% of max. Finish your warm-up with 4 x 60 seconds of skiing at a relaxed not maximal speed.

WORKOUT

Winter activity: Skating or classic skiing on any trail
Summer activity: 10K running time trial
Exerciser: Ski simulator set for 30 minutes of high-intensity work
Distance: 10K at race pace
Time: 30-60 minutes
Effort: RPE 7-8; 85-94% max HR. You need to focus on the task at hand during the pace.

COOL-DOWN: 10 minutes of easy skiing on the flats. Finish with 10 minutes of stretching.

CALORIES BURNED: About 600-900

COMMENTS

A 10K is still a sprint for world class skiers, but it can be a long distance for us lesser mortals. Start at a pace a little slower than you think you can maintain, then pick it up as you feel able. Using a 5K loop is a great way to do this workout. Try to have negative splits; that is, ski faster the second 5K than the first. You'll then be on your way to establishing good pacing.

WORKOUT 4

OVER DISTANCE INTERVALS
TOTAL TIME: 65-100 minutes

4

WARM-UP: 10 minutes of easy skiing on a flat trail, slowly increasing HR up to 75% of max. Finish your warm-up with a few minutes at race pace.

WORKOUT

Winter activity: Skating or classic skiing on a packed, hilly trail
Summer activity: Bike riding to imitate the skiing workout
Exerciser: Ski simulator set to imitate the skiing workout
Distance: 12-24K total, including interval and recovery skiing
Time: 35-100 minutes, alternating 15- to 20-minute intervals at 20K race speed with 3-5 minutes of recovery skiing
Effort: RPE 7; 85-89% max HR during intervals. You need to focus on the task at hand during the pace. RPE 2-3; 60-69% max HR during recovery. When you recover you can tell full stories.

COOL-DOWN: 10 minutes of easy skiing on the flats. Finish with 10 minutes of stretching.

CALORIES BURNED: About 1,200-1,800

COMMENTS

These race speed intervals help you learn pacing for a long race, but with 3- to 5-minute rests. Do the intervals on the same section of the trail each time. Start slowly, then try to increase the speed on subsequent intervals until you find the highest pace you can maintain. Recover to about 65% of max HR before starting the next interval. A really good workout is 2-4 intervals, but you can do more—at a reasonable pace—if you are really feeling good.

WORKOUT 5

5

10K RACE
TOTAL TIME: 65-95 minutes

WARM-UP: 15 minutes of easy skiing on a flat trail, slowly increasing HR up to 75% of max. Finish your warm-up with a few minutes at race pace.

WORKOUT

Winter activity: Skating or classic skiing race

Summer activity: 10K road running race

Exerciser: Ski simulator or rowing machine set for 30 minutes of high-intensity work

Distance: 10K

Time: 30-60 minutes

Effort: RPE 7-8; 85-94% max HR. You need to focus on the task at hand during the pace.

COOL-DOWN: 10 minutes of easy skiing on the flats. Finish with 10 minutes of stretching.

CALORIES BURNED: About 650-950

COMMENTS

Racing requires good pacing and being able to ski as fast as possible without pushing so hard that you exceed your anaerobic threshold and become fatigued too early in the race. Race against your own personal best time. If you always race with the same crowd, figure your time as a percentage of the average of the top three times. That way, you'll be able to assess your improvements even with the changing terrain and snow of each race.

WORKOUT 6

15K RACE
TOTAL TIME: 80-125 minutes

WARM-UP: 15 minutes of easy skiing on a flat trail, slowly increasing HR up to 75% of max. Finish your warm-up with a few minutes at race pace.

WORKOUT

Winter activity: Skating or classic skiing race

Summer activity: Orienteering a cross-country running race with map and compass or any 45- to 60-minute event of your choice

Exerciser: Ski simulator set to imitate a 45-minute, high-intensity, natural interval workout

Distance: 15K

Time: 45-90 minutes

Effort: RPE 7-8; 85-94% max HR. You need to focus on the task at hand during the pace.

COOL-DOWN: 10 minutes of easy skiing on the flats. Finish with 10 minutes of stretching.

CALORIES BURNED: About 900-1,250

COMMENTS

It helps to ski the course the day before the race so you can get an idea of where the hills are and where you need to slow down or surge ahead. Be sure to start at a pace you can maintain. Start slightly slower than for the 10K race, but you should be able to ski from the midway point to the end as fast as you do during the shorter race. Ski races are not won in the sprint off the starting line, but rather through careful use of your optimal speed throughout the event.

30K RACE
TOTAL TIME: 135-225 minutes

WARM-UP: 10 minutes of easy skiing on a flat trail, slowly increasing HR up to 70% of max, then skiing for about 5 minutes at this intensity. These long races usually have a mass start, so you may cool down a lot as you wait in the start with everyone else. If you start cool, use the first 10-15 minutes to slowly get up to speed.

WORKOUT

Winter activity: Skating or classic skiing race

Summer activity: Half marathon running race, half triathlon 2-hour event, or canoe race

Distance: 30K

Time: 100-190 minutes

Effort: RPE 6-7; 80-89% max HR. You can think clearly with some focus needed on uphills.

COOL-DOWN: 10 minutes of easy skiing on the flats. Finish with 10 minutes of stretching.

CALORIES BURNED: About 1,400-1,900

COMMENTS

Ski long-distance races at a slightly slower pace than you ski 10K, 15K, or shorter races. Your fitness level will determine what percentage of max HR you can maintain, so use the talking scale. You should be able to think clearly as you find a pace that is comfortable and easy to maintain. Race organizers usually provide feed stations for 30K races. If they don't, you'll need your own water bottle and energy bars.

WORKOUT 8

50K RACE
TOTAL TIME: 3-6 hours

8

WARM-UP: These long races usually have a mass start, so you may cool down a lot as you wait in the start with everyone else. If you do a hard warm-up and get sweaty, you may get quite chilled waiting for the start. Most racers forego the prerace warm-up and just use the first 10-15 minutes to slowly build their speed as their bodies adjust to the demands.

WORKOUT

Winter activity: Skating or classic skiing race
Summer activity: Marathon running race, triathlon 3-4 hour event, or any other long endurance event
Distance: 50K
Time: 3-6 hours
Effort: RPE 4-7; 70-89% max HR. You can think clearly.

COOL-DOWN: 10 minutes of easy skiing on the flats if possible, then put on a dry top right away or change completely into dry clothes. You may feel like stopping and lying down right after the race. If so, put on dry clothes before you lie down. You need to eat lots of carbohydrates to replenish your body and drink fluids to rehydrate. Stretch well before you tighten up, especially if you have to get in a car and drive.

CALORIES BURNED: About 3,500-5,000

COMMENTS

Just finishing a 50K race is the main challenge for many skiers, while well-trained individuals may cruise along at 90% of max HR for most of the distance. You may need to set a pace not much faster than an easy touring pace. The key is to ski at a speed where you are very comfortable and you are using your energy efficiently. It is important to stay hydrated and to eat small amounts of food frequently during the event.

PART III

TRAINING BY THE WORKOUT ZONES

By now, if you've read through the workouts, you probably have an idea of the varied training possible for cross-country skiing. Obviously, during the snow season, most of the activity is skiing with some running and other fitness activities to keep it interesting. When there is no snow on the ground, cross-country skiers tend to train more like triathletes, using a wide variety of activities, but always remembering that they must train their arms as well as their legs.

This section helps you understand how to put the workouts in part II into a reasonable training plan tailored to fit your needs. The workouts are not intended to be used in order. Workouts are ordered primarily in terms of intensity, and you can also think of the order in terms of how tired you may be when you finish: Workouts become more taxing in each successive zone. Of course, some of the long-distance workouts, even in the Green and Blue zones, may be more taxing than the short intervals, but more on that later.

Chapter 12 includes basic training guidelines that apply to all endurance sports. Chapter 13 outlines sample programs that you can use as presented or modify to meet your specific needs and goals. Chapter 14, which may be the most important in terms of motivation, discusses ways to monitor your training through the use of a simple series of field tests and shows you how to record your training.

The fitness evaluation tests that you took in chapter 3 will give you an idea of what level is appropriate for you to use when starting your training. The sample programs in this book are based on three levels:

- **Basic Fitness and Maintenance.** If your score on the readiness assessment was less than 36 or if your adjusted 1.5-mile run took longer than 13 minutes (males) or 14 minutes (females), this is the place to start. These training programs will use workouts primarily from the low-intensity Green and Blue zones. These workouts will provide the greatest aerobic benefit until you are more fit and ready to begin a few short and easy intervals. If these workouts are too difficult, then shorten them up to a length you can manage. If they seem too easy, consider going just a little harder or, better, adding more distance and time if possible.

- **Moderate Fitness and Improvement.** If your score on the readiness assessment was 37 to 54 or your adjusted 1.5-mile running time was 10 to13 minutes (males) or 11 to 14 minutes (females), you are ready to start with this program. These workouts are for those skiers who are interested in a good level of fitness and in working a little harder and more frequently, possibly with the goal of entering a few citizen races. This level covers a broad range of abilities, with most workouts coming from both the low- and medium-intensity zones and a third of the workouts from the high-intensity zones.

- **Competitive.** If your readiness assessment score was more than 50 and your 1.5-mile running time was faster than 10 minutes (males) or 11 minutes (females), you are probably ready to train using these programs, although you may want to start first with the moderate schedules and then move up when you feel ready. These training plans are for those skiers who like to ski fast, long, and frequently and who might want to do a fair amount of racing. If you are an experienced skier or a very fit athlete getting into cross-country skiing, you will enjoy the challenge of these workouts.

Adjust the training plans to fit your needs and goals. Be sure to read through the following chapter so you understand the basic principles of putting together a training plan before you make major revisions. Keep good records as you experiment. You will soon learn what works best for you.

12

Setting Up Your Program

Athletes have two basic needs: to stay healthy and to train appropriately for positive results. These two goals require a balancing act. If you train *too much* and don't get enough rest and recovery, you may find yourself ill or overtrained (feeling flat and tired). If you don't train *enough,* you won't stimulate training improvements and you may not see many benefits.

General Rules

The general order for all endurance training follows these basic guidelines: Develop the endurance base first with lots of low-intensity activities, add strength, and finally work on speed. If you are very sedentary, start your training by walking more, using stairs instead of elevators whenever possible, mowing the lawn with a push mower instead of a riding tractor, walking your dog, golfing, dancing, and doing other light activities. Walking is a great way to start.

Variety in your training will also keep you enthusiastic and looking forward to your exercise. During the dryland period, it is good to alternate a variety of training activities as well as varying the duration of your workouts and the intensity of each session.

During the winter, ski on different trails, vary the technique that you use, and be sure to change the distances and intensities of your workouts. If possible, include training days of brisk walking or jogging, indoor swimming, or downhill skiing.

If you stick to the following basic principles, you should find a pleasant balance of exercise, variety, and rest for a pleasant and productive training program.

Hard-Easy Principle

Hard training stresses your body, but it is during the recovery periods that your body responds and makes the compensatory improvements. The principle of hard-easy means that between all hard training sessions, or series of hard sessions, you need to have time to recover and to realize the benefits of your training. Hard workouts are relative, but either workout duration or intensity can determine the total stress on your body. Hard days do not necessarily mean high intensity; instead, they refer to how tired you are after the training session or at the end of the day. For a moderately fit individual, a four-hour hike might be much more exhausting than a half-hour series of intervals, even though the intensity of the hike was quite low. Your fitness level also determines how fast you recover and how much stress you need to get a training response.

Hard workouts are relative to your fitness level. Well-trained athletes feel tired for a while after a hard workout, and easy workouts leave them feeling refreshed and recovered. Thus, experienced skiers will use Green and Blue workouts for recovery. Beginners may find even some of the Blue and Green workouts difficult, and stretching and short walks will help speed recovery. For all except the very fit athlete, every hard workout should be followed by at least one day of easy recovery training before the next hard workout. It is important to be rested before intervals and speed workouts if you wish to have good effort and intensity.

Day-Off Rule

The more serious an athlete, the harder it is for him or her to understand that rest is a part of every training program. Plan a day or two off from hard training every week. You may train every day, but a few days each week need to be very easy recovery workouts. If you are less fit, plan at least one or two days off per week from formal training, but stretch and use easy walks to improve your recovery. Skiers who race a lot, usually on the weekends, usually take Mondays off from training, and they often do easy recovery workouts on Tuesdays before getting back into any hard workouts. If you want to train every day, take a couple of days a week for recovery workouts. Easy exercise is better for recovery than inactive rest.

> **TRAINING TIP** In addition to planning days off, listen to your body as you make daily training decisions. Try taking your heart rate while lying quietly in bed each morning. If it is five or more beats per minute higher than normal, consider reducing your workout for that day. You can also check your heart rate during normal daily activities. If you find it to be higher than normal, consider taking the day off from training.

Specificity Principle

By *specificity* I mean "what you do is what you get." Each type of training will give you specific results. If all you do is long, slow, distance training, you will eventually become very good at going a long distance slowly, which incidently is a great way to start a program. If all you do is short, hard workouts, then you'll be able to do short, hard bursts, but you won't be able to maintain the effort for long.

Because of the specificity principle, it is important to understand your goals and then to plan accordingly. Cross-country ski racing takes a blend of endurance and speed, so it is important to have variety in your training to develop a good base for racing: long, slow workouts; short, easy recovery training; a variety of strength workouts; short speed intervals; and some high-intensity training such as long intervals or time trials.

The adage, "If you always do what you've always done, you'll always get what you always got," is true for training as well as life. A wide variety of activities and intensities will keep you interested in training, keep it refreshing, and develop a balance in your health.

Developing Your Aerobic Base

The foundation of all programs is a good aerobic base. This comes from lots of training time spent at easy intensities. The workouts need to last at least 20 minutes for starters, and eventually increase to about 30-45 minutes, with an occasional longer session of one or more hours. These low-intensity activities improve the ability of your muscles to use fats and carbohydrates, both aerobic fuels. Easy activities improve your ability to recover from training and will make you feel better in all of your activities. Easy work also introduces your muscles to new activities without injury.

The aerobic base may be developed through participation in a few or in many aerobic sports at a low intensity. You should be able to talk comfortably with a training partner during low-intensity activities and your breathing will not be strained. Examples of easy aerobic activities include brisk walking, easy jogging, cycling on the road and gentle trails, cross-country ski touring, hiking, swimming, aerobics classes, rope jumping, rowing, and stair climbing. Of course, you can do all of these activities at a higher intensity, but start with a comfortable intensity and a short duration. As you get into better shape, a world of opportunity will await you. Resist the urge to push hard during the early stages of your training.

You'll also see progress in the duration of each training session. When you're just starting, most of the workouts are short—less than 30 minutes. As you get more fit, longer workouts will give you better benefits. Start with short and easy workouts and graduate slowly to longer durations at a low intensity. Eventually you can add higher intensity and speed to your program. The total hours (volume) that you train each week will also increase somewhat as your fitness level rises.

Intervals

The term *intervals* simply means periods of hard intensity followed by periods of recovery. Intervals come in many lengths and intensities. Intervals allow you to spend more time at a chosen intensity by breaking the harder portions of the workout into short segments interspersed with periods of rest.

Intervals are usually broken down into three categories: aerobic, anaerobic, and speed. Each category stresses a different metabolism and using different fuels.

- **Aerobic intervals** allow you to think clearly and focus during the workout. You're not breathing hard, but you can feel some muscle fatigue, especially in the later intervals. The fuel for aerobic intervals is carbohydrates and fatty acids. Aerobic intervals are ideal for teaching you the pace of longer races as well as for developing the efficiency with which your cardiovascular system delivers oxygen and your muscles use oxygen. Aerobic intervals are usually three minutes or longer.
- **Anaerobic intervals** sound hard, but I don't recommend performing them at maximal intensity for ski training. *Anaerobic*

simply means that you are working at an intensity where not all of your power is being produced aerobically. Any time you ski at a faster pace than you can maintain for about 45 minutes, you are probably somewhere slightly above the anaerobic threshold. I recommend that you perform anaerobic intervals at the pace you'd be skiing in the middle of a 5K race. Anaerobic intervals are like skiing a short piece of the race, taking a rest, then doing it again. Using the concept of a race with lots of rests is a nice way to get in lots of race-speed training without hurting much. The fuel for anaerobic intervals is carbohydrates, which result in some lactic acid accumulation. The intensity I suggest for most of these workouts, though, still requires most of the energy to be produced aerobically. These race intensity intervals are the best way to improve your ability to use oxygen so that your body continues to be fueled aerobically instead of anaerobically.

© John Kelly

Intervals are like dancing on snow.

- **Speed intervals** are also anaerobic, but the intensity is maximal and the duration is always very short. These 10- to 30-second intervals use stored adenosine triphosphate (ATP) and creatine phosphate (CP) for their energy needs. All food sources ultimately convert into ATP. Creatine phosphate can quickly replenish the ATP, but both are in short supply and will together last less than two minutes. Speed intervals help you learn how to recruit more muscle fibers and learn the coordination of skiing fast. As your maximal speed increases, your sustainable submaximal race speeds will also increase due to better skiing economy.

A broad mixture of length and intensity of intervals will best prepare you for the demands of cross-country ski racing where the hills require more intensity and you recover on the downhills. Cross-country ski racing doesn't requie a constant energy output, but rather a series of intervals and short rests as you ski up hills and then glide down.

Time Trials and Self-Tests

Periodic trials, mock races against your previous best times, will give you an idea of how you are doing. Find a ski course that you like, preferably close to home. Even better, join a club that hosts regular time trials and check your times against those of your friends to get an idea of how your times are improving relative to theirs. Be aware of changing conditions that might affect your time.

Time trials help you practice racing. Think of them as real races, and use them to learn how to pace yourself and to get over the pre-race jitters. For important races you might consider doing a time trial on the course, or at least on a portion of the course. You should keep your time trials to less than 30 minutes in length.

Adjusting Your Schedule to Your Needs

You will need to adjust your training program as your fitness improves. At first, slightly increase the amount of easy distance that you ski, then add in a little more intensity to the distance workouts. Eventually, you can increase or decrease the number or intensity of your intervals. (It is usually better to increase the number and length of intervals rather than the intensity.)

If you find yourself tired after a combination of workouts, consider adding an extra rest day into your schedule. Be sure to pay attention to the messages that your body gives you. If you are scheduled for a hard set of Orange intervals, but are still tired from the previous day, consider doing a recovery Green workout instead, or do fewer intervals with more easy skiing.

Each of us has our own strengths and weaknesses. You'll find a set of field tests in chapter 14 that will help you evaluate individual strengths and weaknesses. If you learn that your legs don't have much power or that your arms could use some work, adjust your program by adding exercises that will do more in those areas.

The Yearly Program

We all need breaks and variation in our daily schedules along with a sense of stability and continuity. Training can give you that daily break, but you need to develop it as a predictable part of your routine. Within your training routine, learn to include variation in the type of exercise, the duration, and the intensity so you can stay motivated and excited about fitness.

Cross-country skiing lends itself wonderfully to either a 12-month training cycle in which different periods of the year emphasize specific training or to a program allowing for a competitive summer sport season and a winter cross-country season.

The idea of *periodization,* or cycled training, has been well developed and is almost universally accepted. All high-level athletes understand that their training year needs to be broken down into different training periods with different goals. Here are the four basic stages of a yearly aerobic training program:

- **Recovery period.** This may last from one to one-and-a-half months, usually right after the competitive season.
- **Basic endurance period.** This three- to four-month period during the off-season may also include strength and technique work.
- **Speed endurance period.** This three- to four-month preseason tune-up period is often called the precompetition period. It develops speed, power, and endurance.
- **Competition.** This two- to three-month period is a time of reduced training, some increase in intervals, and lots of recovery to be well rested for competitions. If you don't race, then what would normally be the competition season can be a great time to get in lots of skiing.

It is possible to cut the length of each period in half for a summer competitive season in one sport and a winter competitive season in cross-country skiing. You may not achieve the same high results with two seasons a year that you would if you trained for only one, but you may love the competition and the training for multiple sports.

Recovery Period

Following a period of competitions, it is important for all athletes to give their body a rest. There is good evidence that detraining for a brief period after competition helps athletes come back the next year and achieve higher results than if they maintained their fitness year 'round.

The recovery period usually starts after the final races of the season and lasts a month to a month and a half. For most skiers, recovery takes place in the later part of March through April. During this time you may stay active but will follow no specific training plan and have no hard activities. Do some easy activities such as walking, hiking, light cycling, and other relaxing activities. This is a time to let your body regenerate. Stay active, but let yourself decline out of racing shape. For those of you following the easy and moderate programs, continue to stay active, but try different activities for a refreshing break.

Basic Endurance Period

All aerobic programs initiate their year by building an aerobic base. For skiers, this means that during the summer months, usually May through August, you'll do a lot of easy distance training with only a few intervals for pace training and endurance.

The basic endurance period is also a good time to work on strength training if this is a limiting factor for you. If you wish to incorporate a strength program into your cross-country ski training, work with an instructor who is knowledgeable about strength development for aerobic activities.

Speed Endurance Period

Racing, and improving your anaerobic threshold, requires speed and interval training. The basic fitness program never gets to these more difficult workouts, but the moderate- and high-level programs incorporate more intensity into these months of speed and endurance training, usually September through December. You'll maintain high volume and you'll do more intervals. There are also more very long workouts and cycles where you will have high volume plus lots of intensity training. Look ahead and evaluate the entire month. Be sure to precede hard weeks with easier ones.

Competition Period

This is a time to go very fast during races and intervals along with going very slow for the rest of your skiing. When you're not racing, you'll probably be recovering to race. The programs I outline for the

© John Kekky

If you are feeling good, or simply want to ski more, go ahead and enjoy the snow.

recovery period have a low overall volume of training with a high percentage of time spent at higher racing or interval intensities. Most of the major cross-country ski races in North America happen in January and February, with a few large races continuing into early March.

Pay attention to your health and how you feel. If necessary, reduce the amount of training. If you are feeling good and know that you can handle more training, or simply want to ski more, go ahead and enjoy the snow.

Weekly and Monthly Variations

The concept of periodization also works in microcycles, or shorter periods of time than the four big periods of the year. Within each month, alternate weeks that are hard overall with weeks that are easier.

Preceding hard weeks, or weeks with competition, it is nice to have easier weeks during which you prepare for the greater stress to come.

Within each week, you will also need to vary the activities using the hard-easy rule so that you have recovery before and after hard workouts. I've followed this principle when devising the competitive program in the next chapter. The competitive program often contains two difficult days back to back, but those are always followed by an easier recovery period.

Apply these basic concepts to your training:

- Vary the muscle groups you work on from day to day.
- Vary the intensity of the workouts from day to day.
- If you do two workouts a day, stress different systems or different parts of your body.
- If you do two workouts a day, separate them by as much time as possible.

13

Sample Skiing Programs

In this chapter are sample programs for the three levels of fitness I have identified. You can set up your own training schedule by following the guidelines in the previous chapter, or you can rely on the sample programs here. For the moderate fitness and improvement program and the competitive program, I give sample schedules for different periods of the year. As you improve in your fitness, you will find that you may want to move up to a harder program. Be patient in your training. All good things take time.

Basic Fitness and Maintenance Program

These programs are for general fitness and for those who would like to enjoy ski touring and a healthy lifestyle built around aerobic exercise. There is only one four-week example. You can repeat it with your own modifications, or you can graduate to the moderate fitness and improvement level.

The activities in this program are almost all from the Blue and Green zones, and most are easy intensity with a few longer workouts during the final week.

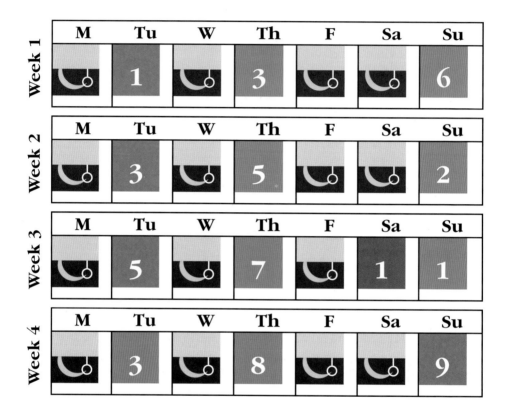

A new cross-country skier, just learning to glide.

TRAINING TIP I train most consistently when I have a set routine that fits my work and family schedule. Within that routine, I vary the location, intensity, method, and duration of my workouts. I think most skiers do this.

Moderate Fitness and Improvement Program

Once you have developed a base of aerobic fitness you are ready to participate in a program that can bring you to a higher level. This program includes all of the zones except the Red zone. The primary goals are to help you improve your aerobic fitness and develop better muscular power and endurance. This program will also prepare you for racing in a few citizen races.

It is best not to increase the intensity or the length of any of these workouts until you feel comfortable doing all of those listed here.

The program is broken into two segments: basic endurance, usually for the summer months and early fall, and speed endurance, which takes place in the late fall and winter. If you want to do a race or two, plan your program so you finish the fourth week of the speed endurance program seven days before the race, then use the first week of the speed endurance program to lead up to your race.

Basic Endurance Period

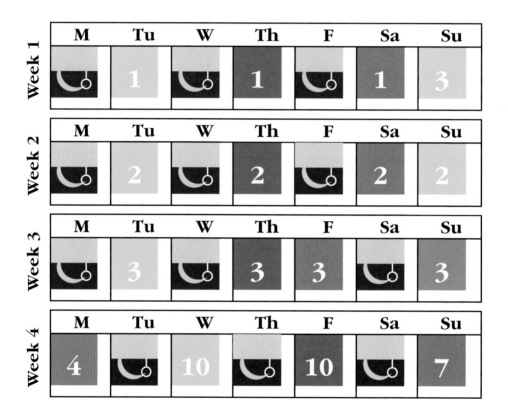

Speed Endurance Period

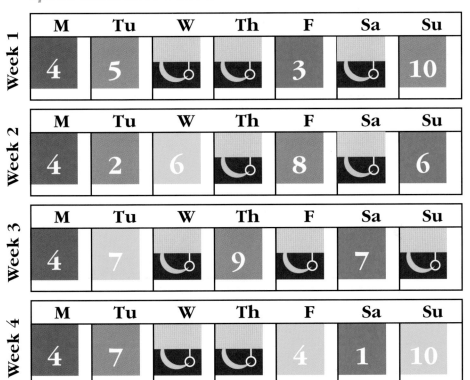

© Richard Etchberger

Long slow distance skis require taking food and drink
along as you enjoy hours of easy skiing.

Competitive Program

This program is for those athletes who have achieved a high level of
skiing fitness and skill. It is extremely important to listen to the signals that your body is giving to you and to make appropriate adjustments in this training program.

This program combines higher volumes of aerobic base training
during the basic endurance period (May through September). The
speed and intervals increase during the speed endurance period
(October through December) so that you are doing both high volume and high intensity at times. The competitive season (January
through March) combines reduced volume with speed and recovery
for optimal racing. If you want to ski more kilometers during the
competitive season, go ahead, but reduce your intensity somewhat
and try to take it easy for a few days before races.

This program looks intimidating with training often scheduled for
six days a week. However, you will find that many of the workouts
are low intensity and are recommended to enhance recovery. These

easy workouts can be replaced with easy walking, or even stretching. Mondays and Fridays of each week are often strength training, which can be dropped if you feel you have adequate strength and replaced with basic endurance skiing. The other option is to do the circuit strength training in conjunction with one of the other workouts if you need more days off.

Basic Endurance Period (Competitive Program)

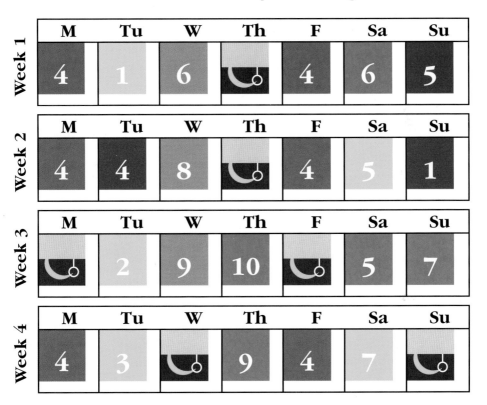

Speed Endurance Period (Competitive Program)

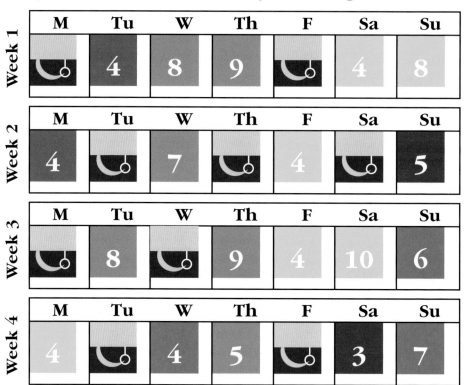

Competition Period (Competitive Program)

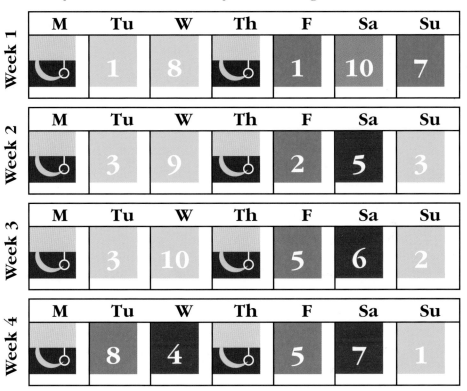

Once you try these suggested programs, you may realize that no one program fits all. You will probably find that you need to make modifications to fit the time you have available, your fitness level, and the types of activities you most enjoy. I encourage you to explore further to learn how to make individual adjustments to your personal program.

Participation in local citizen cross-country ski races is a great way to meet new skiers and have a great time.

Training and exercise are wonderful stimulants, and many athletes "race to train"—the exercise and the training is what they most enjoy. Many others (myself included) want the most benefits with the most economical use of their time. However you would categorize yourself, you need to be able to measure your progress and get feedback that your training is effective. The following chapter should help you monitor your progress and help you to adjust your personal program so that it best fits you.

14

Charting Your Progress

The process of training can aptly be summed up by the phrase, "It's hard to get where you're going if you don't know where you are." Charting your progress by keeping records allows you to know what you have done in the past, keep track of goals, evaluate what you are doing, and then to make the necessary changes to be more effective the next time.

Testing is another method to help evaluate the effectiveness of a training program. For many sports it is simple to go out and do a time trial or a race to see if your training is helping you get better. Cross-country skiing, however, presents a special problem. For much of the year, there is no snow, so it's hard to know how effective your training is. Additionally, race results for any sport don't necessarily tell you what you need to know to improve your training. It is often necessary to look at individual components and needs of a sport such as strength, speed, and endurance of specific muscle groups and see if you can measure each component to evaluate your adequacy in those areas. This chapter provides a series of tests to help you determine your progress. Progress requires having goals and sticking to a program.

TRAINING TIP Before starting a training program, set goals for yourself and visualize yourself reaching those goals. Write your goals down and put them where you will see them frequently. This will help you to stick to your program.

Sticking to Your Program

Experience and research has shown that 50 percent of people that start an exercise program will quit within the first six months. Here are some ideas to help you avoid becoming a dropout:

- Schedule your training time at the beginning of each week.
- Make training a routine that you are comfortable with.
- Become part of a club or program.
- Train with others who have similar goals.
- Train at a level that is comfortable to you.
- Be sure your family and friends understand your goals and support you.
- Find times for exercise that are convenient for you and your family.
- Minimize travel time and use it for training instead of for driving.
- Get used to training in all weather. Many athletes fondly remember a day of hiking in the rain, for example. Another alternative is to use indoor equipment when the weather outside is bad.
- Keep your schedule varied.
- Set goals for training duration and distances.
- Update your goals each time you get close to your current goals.

Setting Goals

Many books on sport psychology are available, and they all agree on the need for athletes to set goals and to move toward attaining them. Goals can give us drive. When setting goals, remember that the journey is in the movement toward the goal. If you reach the goal or get near it, it is time to reevaluate and reset the goal. Here are a few guidelines for goal setting:

- Keep your goals challenging but realistic. This is the hardest task. If you set long-term goals with short steps along the way, the road may be a little easier.

© Mountain Stock/John Clausen

Skiing with your family is a wonderful family outing and can help to guide your children towards a lifetime of aerobic enjoyment.

- Try to avoid setting time limits on your goals. Let your body dictate your progress. Pushing too hard to reach a goal may result in injury.
- Visualize the rewards of reaching the goal. See yourself on the victory podium or standing on a weight scale looking at your new target weight. See yourself skiing with grace and agility over a wintry trail. Try to imagine the goal and all of its end results as you move toward it.
- Be specific about your goals. Set goals that you can measure and evaluate.
- Base goals on your own performance, not on the outcome of races where you have no control over the performance of others.
- Write your goals down and look at them periodically.

Visions are powerful, and goals are your vision of what you want to become. Begin to treat yourself as the new person that you are becoming and you will be on your way.

Evaluating Your Training Progress

Periodic testing provides great feedback to athletes of any ability. Testing allows you to evaluate the effectiveness of your training and to monitor progress, or lack of it. Through field testing, you can identify some of the weaknesses that might limit your performance in cross-country skiing. By comparing your performance with a group average of your peers, you can get a rough estimate of muscle groups and performance criteria that need more specific training. Most important, periodic field testing provides feedback that will help keep you motivated and allow you to set very specific training goals. These field tests give you a way to check your progress toward your goals.

In the pages that follow, I introduce you to a simple series of field tests you can use during the spring, summer, and fall (and winter if you have access to indoor facilities), to help you evaluate different components of your training. By repeating the tests over time, you can monitor your training by comparing current test results with prior results. If there is no improvement in some of the tests, then the training is providing only maintenance and might need to be adjusted if your goal is to improve.

This battery of tests can be performed bimonthly during the summer and fall. When snow is on the ground, continue with those tests that you can do indoors. Testing through the race season is extremely interesting and will help motivate you to maintain your training. Never forget, however, that the most important field test is the actual race. The battery of tests that follows is useful in evaluating components of a skier's performance, but each test alone is not an indicator of final performance.

There are eight tests. The first one should be done on a separate day from the other seven. The seven remaining tests should be performed in order. Many of the tests are easier to perform with the help of a partner. If you have a regular training partner, perform the tests with his or her help. If you don't, enlist a friend to help you. Warm up for each day's tests by doing an easy 15-minute hike or jog with poles.

The criteria noted with each test were developed with master skiers (adults over 30) participating in our Team Birke ski programs.

If your results on any test put you in the "Adequate" category, you can definitely handle the easy ski touring and easy training of the Green and Blue zones. You may find a few tests where you do not reach the "Adequate" range. Don't let that stop you from skiing. Instead, think of your score as an indication that you have great potential for improvement in that area and consider it to be a good area to focus some training. For better fitness and racing, your goals should be to get into the "Good" or "Excellent" categories on most tests. Focus on those areas where you are weakest and maintain your strengths.

1) 1.5-Mile Run

See chapter 3 for details of the 1.5-mile run/walk test and for a table to evaluate your results.

2) 10-Hop Test

This is a test of leg power and explosiveness. Stretch out a 100-foot tape measure on a level surface with good footing, or put markers every 5 feet. Grass is an acceptable surface if it's dry. Mark yourself a start line at the beginning of the tape. Back up to get a running start, and when you get to the start line, begin long bounds, alternating feet. Bound as far as you can with each stride. Your distance is best noted by a spotter at the end of the tenth bound. If you have been very sedentary or have other difficulties bounding on one leg, skip this test and work with a strength trainer to begin a leg strength program. *Note.* You should continue to bound and slow down gradually. Don't attempt to stop abruptly at the end of the tenth bound. You can adjust your results by adding half a foot for every year over 30.

NORMS FOR 10-HOP TEST		
Category	**Males**	**Females**
World class	>90 feet	>80 feet
Excellent	70–90 feet	57–80 feet
Very good	55–69 feet	46–56 feet
Good	40–54 feet	32–45 feet
Adequate for easy skiing	35–39 feet	27–31 feet

3) Towel Pull-Ups

For this arm and forearm strength test, loop a sturdy old towel over a tree branch or other support. Grab each end of the towel with one hand. From a hanging position do as many pull-ups as possible, bringing your chin up to your hands and then going back to a nearly straight arm hang. Most people don't use their arms much in activities of daily living, and if you are not able to do any pull-ups, don't feel alone—you are part of the majority. If you score low on this test, start by standing on a stool, grab the towel and slowly lower yourself, and then try to come back up as far as you can. Do multiple repeats of lowering yourself. This is eccentric (lengthening) strength training and can provide good results. Another option is to have a partner assist your pull-ups by supporting some of your body weight as you lift yourself.

NORMS FOR TOWEL PULL-UP TEST		
Category	**Males**	**Females**
World class	20+	16+
Excellent	15-19	10-15
Good	8-14	6-9
Adequate for easy skiing	0-7	0-5

4) Super Skier Test

For this test of back strength, lie on your stomach with your arms stretched out in front. Time how long you can keep your arms, shoulders, knees, and toes off of the ground. This isn't a good

NORMS FOR SUPER SKIER TEST	
World class	>3 minutes
Excellent	1-3 minutes
Good	45-60 seconds
Adequate for easy skiing	20-45 seconds

test for people with back injuries or a history of back problems. If you have a bad back, develop a good routine to maintain back health. Men and women score equally on this test.

Super skier test.

5) Pole Touches

This is a test of leg abduction power and flexibility. Clearly mark two lines (you can use two ski poles) three meters apart (9 feet 10 inches). Stand in the middle between the poles with your feet parallel to the poles. For one minute, run side to side to touch the ground with both hands outside of one pole, then sprint to the other side to touch the ground outside of the other pole. Count how many alternating touches you can do with both hands touching the ground outside of the poles.

NORMS FOR POLE TOUCH TEST		
Category	**Males**	**Females**
World class	50 or more	45 or more
Excellent	40-49	32-44
Good	30-39	24-31
Adequate for easy skiing	15-29	12-23

Adjustments: Give yourself one extra touch for each 3 years you are over 30. Give yourself one extra touch for each two inches you are below six feet.

6) Bench Dips

This is a test of triceps, shoulder, and latissimus dorsi muscular strength and endurance. Use two picnic tables or chairs. Situate your hands on the edge of one table (or chair) and support your feet at an equal height. Lower your body down to the point that your upper arm is parallel with the ground. Your elbows should point behind you rather than pointing out to the side of the body. Push yourself back up. Keep going until you can't do anymore. Count how many you can do before fatigue stops you.

NORMS FOR BENCH DIP TEST

Category	Males	Females
World class	>125	>125
Excellent	75–124	70–124
Very good	40–75	35–69
Average	25–39	18–34
Adequate for easy skiing	10–24	5–17

© Dennis G. Hendricks

Bench dips.

7) Bent Knee Sit-Ups

This is a test of your abdominal and hip flexor power and endurance. Lie on the floor on your back and flex your knees to 90 degrees, cross your arms over your chest, and put your hands on your shoulders. Brace your feet firmly under a sofa or have a partner hold them. Time yourself for two full minutes and count only those sit-ups where you touch your legs with your elbows without your hands coming off of your shoulders.

NORMS FOR BENT KNEE SIT-UPS TEST

Category	Males	Females
World class	>120	>110
Excellent	80–119	70–109
Very good	60–79	55–69
Good	40–59	35–54
Adequate for easy skiing	25–39	20–34

Adjustments: Add one sit-up for every 2 years over 30.

8) Box (or Pole) Jump

Doing the box jump requires building a strong box or finding a suitable bench 10 to 14 inches wide and 12 inches (for females) or 14 inches (for males) high. You could also use a rope or pole suspended 12 or 14 inches above the ground. For every 10 years you are older than 30, remove one inch in height from the box or pole.

For the box jump, start on the top of the box facing forward and first jump down to the left of the box, then back to the top, to the right side, and back to the top. Continue jumping to alternate sides. Each touch on the top of the box counts as one jump. Count your jumps for two minutes. You will probably fatigue before the full two minutes.

For the pole or rope jump, jump sideways back and forth over the suspended rope or pole. Count your touches on each side of the rope or pole for two minutes—again, expect to fatigue before then. For both tests, if you fatigue and cannot maintain a good rhythm you may rest and restart any time during the two minutes, but the clock keeps going.

NORMS FOR BOX (OR POLE) HOP TEST

Category	Box Jump		Rope/Pole Jump	
	Male	Female	Male	Female
World class	>150	>140	>160	>150
Excellent	130-149	120-139	140-159	130-149
Good	80-129	70-119	85-139	75-129
Moderate	45-79	35-69	50-84	40-74
Adequate for easy skiing	20-44	12-34	33-49	16-39

Box jump.

© Steven Gaskill

Keep good records and these tests will be of great benefit to your training by helping you focus on your goals and keeping you motivated.

Keeping Records

Cross-country skiing presents difficulties in measuring performance because your skiing speed will change from course to course with different snow conditions, with different wax, at different temperatures, and even as the humidity changes. Thus, pace is not always a great measure of progress. As I said before, the field tests will give you a great way to evaluate strengths and weaknesses and to see improvement in specific areas of your training. Here are some ideas to help you chart your progress.

- Keep a chart of your field test results. Try to do the tests at least every two to three months.
- Keep track of the times it takes you to run, hike, walk, paddle, or ski specific trails or loops at different RPE intensities. You can check on your improvements in each training activity.
- For strength training, keep track of the resistance for each activity and reward yourself as you see improvements.
- For cross-country racing, chart your time as a percentage of the average of the times of the top three to five racers for a relative comparison of how you are doing against a group of other skiers. Or, select three to five skiers who are your common competitors in most of your races and compare your time to the average of their times. Of course, you can't be sure if they are also improving or declining, but an average will help to eliminate some of the variability.

Keeping a training log is also a very effective motivator and will help you to keep a schedule. You may make copies of the training log sheet on page 167 and keep them in a binder. Each sheet is designed to handle one week of training. The bottom two rows allow you to total the hours that you trained in each zone for the week and for the year. When doing the year totals, you must designate a point as the beginning of your training year. Most skiers begin their training logs at the beginning of May, but any date will work fine.

Record time, rather than distance, as the training criteria. With so many different training modes, it is impossible to compare the distances. There is, however, a column for distance skied. Like any sport, the more that you participate, the more proficient you will become. In this book I've given you recommendations to help you set up your own program, along with sample programs you can use as written. Now the training is up to you. Set your goals and have a great journey discovering the wonders of cross-country skiing.

© John Kelly

Your skiing speed will change with different snow conditions and terrain—keep this in mind when comparing your performance during different workouts.

Date	Weight	Average HR	Training time in each zone		Distance	Comments
			Blue/ Green	Purple/ Yellow	Orange/ Red		
M							
Tu							
W							
Th							
F							
Sa							
Su							
	Totals for week						
	Totals for year to date						

Summary _____

_____

_____

About the Author

Steve Gaskill worked for the U.S. Ski Team for 10 years—as head coach of the Nordic Combined (ski jumping and cross-country skiing) and Cross-Country teams and as director of the coaches' educational programs. Gaskill has coached at three Olympic Games, and twenty skiers who have trained under him have competed in the Olympics. In 1992 the U.S. Ski Association named him the U.S. Cross-Country Coach of the Year.

Gaskill was the founder and first director of Team Birke Ski Education Foundation, which is dedicated to the development of excellence in cross-country ski programs for skiers of all ages. He also has published more than 200 articles about cross-country skiing and has produced six instructional videotapes. He has presented his extensive research findings on training for cross-country skiing to the American College of Sports Medicine and has written a major article for *Medicine and Science in Sports and Exercise*.

Gaskill lives in Burnsville, Minnesota, with his wife, Kathy. His favorite leisure activities include cross-country skiing, hiking, and mountaineering.

Experience the outdoors like never before

SNOWSHOEING

Sally Edwards and Melissa McKenzie
1995 • Paper • 128 pp • Item PEDW0767
ISBN 0-87322-767-0 • $13.95 ($19.50 Canadian)

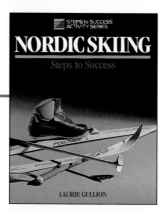

NORDIC SKIING

Steps to Success
Laurie Gullion, MS
1993 • Paper • 160 pp • Item PGUL0394
ISBN 0-87322-394-2 • $14.95 ($21.95 Canadian)

HIGH-PERFORMANCE SKIING

(Second Edition)
John Yacenda and Tim Ross
1997 • Paper • Approx 248 pp • Item PYAC0713
ISBN 0-88011-713-3 • $17.95 ($26.95 Canadian)

Human Kinetics
The Premier Publisher for Sports & Fitness
http://www.humankinetics.com/

Prices are subject to change.